Heritage Builders

Money Matters
Family Night Tool Chest

Creating Lasting Impressions for the Next Generation

Jim Weidmann with
Allen and Lauree Burkett
Adapted from materials by Larry Burkett

Chariot Victor Publishing
A Division of Cook Communications

To all parents who are endeavoring to pass on to your children a godly heritage, we dedicate this book in the Heritage Builders series. We are thrilled to join you in creating lasting impressions for the next generation.

— Allen and Lauree Burkett

Chariot Victor Publishing
a division of Cook Communications, Colorado Springs, Colorado 80918
Cook Communications, Paris, Ontario
Kingsway Communications, Eastbourne, England.

HERITAGE BUILDERS/FAMILY NIGHT TOOL CHEST—MONEY MATTERS
Copyright © 1998 by Heritage Builders Inc., adapted from MONEY MATTERS FOR KIDS™.
Copyright © 1998 by Lauree and Allen Burkett. All rights reserved.

First edition 1998

Edited by Steve Parolini
Design by Bill Gray
Cover and Interior Illustrations by Guy Wolek

ISBN 1-56476-736-1

Printed and bound in the United States of America
02 01 00 99 98   5 4 3 2 1

Heritage Builders/Family Night Tool Chest—Money Matters is a Heritage Builders book, created in association with the authors Lauree and Allen Burkett of MONEY MATTERS FOR KIDS™. To contact Heritage Builders Association, send e-mail to: Hbuilders@aol.com. To contact Money Matters For Kids™, send e-mail to: mail@mmforkids.org or write to their address below.

Money Matters for Kids™
Teaching Kids to Manage God's Gifts
Lauree and Allen Burkett are the cofounders of Money Matters for Kids™. God has planted in their hearts the commitment to see the next generation grounded in God's Word and living His principles. The vision of Money Matters for Kids™ is to provide children and teens with the tools they need to understand the biblical principles of stewardship and to encourage them to live by those principles.
Visit our Web site at: www.mmforkids.org. We welcome your comments and suggestions.
Money Matters for Kids
Lynden, Washington 98264-9760

Contents

Family Nights about Money Matters

The Heritage Builders Series

This resource was created as an outreach of the Heritage Builders Association—a network of families and churches committed to passing a strong heritage to the next generation. Designed to motivate and assist families as they become intentional about the heritage passing process, this series draws upon the collective wisdom of parents, grandparents, church leaders, and family life experts, in an effort to provide balanced, biblical parenting advice along with effective, practical tools for family living. This *Money Matters Family Night Tool Chest* book was created in association with. Allen and Lauree Burkett, cofounders of MONEY MATTERS FOR KIDS™. Their vision is to provide children and teens with the tools they need to understand the biblical principle of stewardship . . . time, talents, material resources, and to encourage them to live by these principles.

Kurt Bruner, M.A.
Executive Editor
Heritage Builders Series

ⓔ Foreword

I truly believe the need to teach children solid, biblical principles of money management is critical to their very survival.

Statistics clearly demonstrate that financial mismanagement is the leading contributor to divorce, emotional problems, and spiritual anemia among young families, and it's getting worse, not better. God's Word clearly details the proper course to follow to avoid financial bondage, and I am proud that Allen and Lauree Burkett have taken up the challenge to teach the next generation God's eternal principles.

I commend Jim Weidmann, Kurt Bruner, and Chariot Victor Publishing for compiling the Heritage Builders Series. I recommend this fine publication to all parents who seek God's best for themselves and their children. The investment of time in teaching these concepts to the young generation will pay dividends for an eternity.

Larry Burkett
Founder and CEO
Christian Financial Concepts

⊚ Introduction

There is toothpaste all over the plastic-covered table. Four young kids are having the time of their lives squeezing the paste out of the tube—trying to expunge every drop like Dad told them to. "Okay," says Dad, slapping a twenty-dollar bill onto the table. "The first person to get the toothpaste back into their tube gets this money!" Little hands begin working to shove the peppermint pile back into rolled-up tubes—with very limited success.

Jim is in the midst of a weekly routine in the Weidmann home when he and his wife spend time creating "impression points" with the kids. "We can't do it, Dad!" protests the youngest child.

"The Bible tells us that's just like your tongue. Once the words come out, it's impossible to get them back in. You need to be careful what you say because you may wish you could take it back." An unforgettable impression is made.

Impression points occur every day of our lives. Intentionally or not, we impress upon our children our values, preferences, beliefs, quirks, and concerns. It happens both through our talk and through our walk. When we do it right, we can turn them on to the things we believe. But when we do it wrong, we can turn them off to the values we most hope they will embrace. The goal is to find ways of making this reality work for us, rather than against us. How? By creating and capturing opportunities to impress upon the next generation our values and beliefs. In other words, through what we've labeled impression points.

The kids are all standing at the foot of the stairs. Jim is at the top of that same staircase. They wait eagerly for Dad's instructions.

"I'll take you to Baskin-Robbins for ice cream if you can figure how to get up here." He has the attention of all four kids. "But there are a few rules. First, you can't touch the stairs. Second, you can't touch the railing. Now, begin!"

After several contemplative moments, the youngest speaks up. "That's impossible, Dad! How can we get to where you are without

touching the stairs or the railing?"

After some disgruntled agreement from two of the other children, Jacob gets an idea. "Hey, Dad. Come down here." Jim walks down the stairs. "Now bend over while I get on your back. Okay, climb the stairs."

Bingo! Jim proceeds to parallel this simple game with how it is impossible to get to God on our own. But when we trust Christ's completed work on our behalf, we can get to heaven. A lasting impression is made. After a trip up the stairs on Dad's back, the whole gang piles into the minivan for a double scoop of mint-chip.

Six years ago, Jim and his wife Janet began setting aside time to intentionally impress upon the kids their values and beliefs through a weekly ritual called "family night." They play games, talk, study, and do the things which reinforce the importance of family and faith. It is during these times that they intentionally create these impression points with their kids. The impact? The kids are having fun and a heritage is being passed.

☙ intentional or "oops"?

Sometimes, we accidentally impress the wrong things on our kids rather than intentionally impressing the right things. But there is an effective, easy way to change that. Routine family nights are a powerful tool for creating intentional impression points with our children.

The concept behind family nights is rooted in a biblical mandate summarized in Deuteronomy 6:5-9.

> *"Love the LORD your God with all your heart and with all your soul and with all your strength. These commandments that I give you today are to be upon your hearts. Impress them on your children."*
> ***How?***
> *"Talk about them when you sit at home and when you walk along the road, when you lie down and when you get up. Tie them as symbols on your hands and bind them on your foreheads. Write them on the doorframes of your houses and on your gates."*

In other words, we need to take advantage of every opportunity to impress our beliefs and values in the lives of our children. A growing network of parents are discovering family nights to be a highly effective, user-friendly approach to doing just that. As one father put it ,"This has changed our entire family life." And another dad, "Our investment of time and energy into family nights has more eternal value than we may ever know." Why? Because they are intentionally teaching their children at the wisdom level, the level at which the children understand and can apply eternal truths.

☙ truth is a treasure

Two boys are running all over the house, carefully following the complex and challenging instructions spelled out on the "truth treasure map" they received moments ago. An earlier map contained a few rather simple instructions that were much easier to follow. But the "false treasure box" it led to left something to be desired. It was empty. Boo Dad! They hope for a better result with map number two.

STEP ONE:

Walk sixteen paces into the front family room.

STEP TWO:

Spin around seven times, then walk down the stairs.

STEP THREE:

Run backward to the other side of the room.

STEP FOUR:

Try and get around Dad and climb under the table.

You get the picture. The boys are laughing at themselves, complaining to Dad, and having a ball. After twenty minutes of treasure hunting they finally reach the elusive "truth treasure box." Little hands open the lid, hoping for a better result this time around. They aren't disappointed. The box contains a nice selection of their favorite candies. Yea Dad!

"Which map was easier to follow?" Dad asks.

"The first one," comes their response.

"Which one was better?"

"The second one. It led to a true treasure," says the oldest.

"That's just like life," Dad shares, "Sometimes it's easier to follow what is false. But it is always better to seek and follow what is true."

They read from Proverbs 2 about the hidden treasure of God's truth and end their time repeating tonight's jingle—"It's best for you to seek what's true." Then they indulge themselves with a mouthful of delicious candy!

☺ the power of family nights

The power of family nights is twofold. First, it creates a formal setting within which Dad and Mom can intentionally instill beliefs, values, or character qualities within their child. Rather than defer to the influence of peers and media, or abdicate character training to the school and church, parents create the opportunity to teach their children the things that matter most.

The second impact of family nights is perhaps even more significant than the first. Twenty to sixty minutes of formal fun and instruction can set up countless opportunities for informal reinforcement. These informal impression points do not have to be created, they just happen—at the dinner table, while driving in the car, while watching television, or any other parent/child time together. Once you have formally discussed a given family night topic, you and your children will naturally refer back to those principles during the routine dialogues of everyday life.

If the truth were known, many of us hated family devotions while growing up. We had them sporadically at best, usually whenever our parents were feeling particularly guilty. But that was fine, since the only thing worse was a trip to the dentist. Honestly, do we really think that is what God had in mind when He instructed us to teach our children? As an alternative, many parents are discovering family nights to be a wonderful complement to or replacement for family devotions as a means of passing their beliefs and values to the kids. In fact, many parents hear their kids ask at least three times per week:

"Can we have family night tonight?"

Music to Dad's and Mom's ears!

@ Keys to Effective Family Nights

There are several keys which should be incorporated into effective family nights.

MAKE IT FUN!

Enjoy yourself, and let the kids have a ball. They may not remember everything you say, but they will always cherish the times of laughter—and so will you.

KEEP IT SIMPLE!

The minute you become sophisticated or complicated, you've missed the whole point. Don't try to create deeply profound lessons. Just try to reinforce your values and beliefs in a simple, easy-to-understand manner. Read short passages, not long, drawn-out sections of Scripture. Remember: The goal is to keep it simple.

DON'T DOMINATE!

You want to pull them into the discovery process as much as possible. If you do all the talking, you've missed the mark. Ask questions, give assignments, invite participation in every way possible. They will learn more when you involve all of their senses and emotions.

GO WITH THE FLOW!

It's fine to start with a well-defined outline, but don't kill spontaneity by becoming overly structured. If an incident or question leads you in a different direction, great! Some of the best impression opportunities are completely unplanned and unexpected.

MIX IT UP!

Don't allow yourself to get into a rut or routine. Keep the sense of excitement and anticipation through variety. Experiment to discover what works best for your family. Use books, games, videos, props, made-up stories, songs, music or music videos, or even go on a family outing.

DO IT OFTEN!

We tend to find time for the things that are really important. It is best to set aside one evening per week (the same evening if possible) for family night. Remember, repetition is the best teacher. The more impressions you can create, the more of an impact you will make.

MAKE A MEMORY!

Find ways to make the lesson stick. For example, just as advertisers create "jingles" to help us remember their products, it is helpful to create family night "jingles" to remember the main theme—such as "It's best for you to seek what's true" or "Just like air, God is there!"

USE OTHER TOOLS FROM THE HERITAGE BUILDERS TOOL CHEST!

Family night is only one exciting way for you to intentionally build a loving heritage for your family. You'll also want to use these other exciting tools from Heritage Builders.

The Family Fragrance: There are five key qualities to a healthy family fragrance, each contributing to an environment of love in the home. It's easy to remember the Fragrance Five by fitting them into an acrostic using the word "Aroma"—

A—Affection
R—Respect
O—Order
M—Merriment
A—Affirmation

Impression Points: Ways that we impress on our children our values, preferences, and concerns. We do it through our talk and our actions. We do it intentionally (through such methods as Family Nights), and we do it incidentally.

The Right Angle: The Right Angle is the standard of normal healthy living against which our children will be able to measure their atttitudes, actions, and beliefs.

Traditions: Meaningful activities which the process of passing on emotional, spiritual, and relational inheritance between generations. Family traditions can play a vital role in this process.

Please see the back of the book for information on how to receive the FREE Heritage Builders Newsletter which contains more information about these exciting tools! Also, look for the new book, *The Heritage,* available at your local Christian bookstore.

How to Use This Tool Chest

Summary page: For those who like the bottom line, we have provided a summary sheet at the start of each family night session. This abbreviated version of the topic briefly highlights the goal, key Scriptures, activity overview, main points, and life slogan. On the reverse side of this detachable page there is space provided for you to write down any ideas you wish to add or alter as you make the lesson your own.

Step-by-step: For those seeking suggestions and directions for each step in the family night process, we have provided a section which walks you through every activity, question, Scripture reading, and discussion point. Feel free to follow each step as written as you conduct the session, or read through this portion in preparation for your time together.

À la carte: We strongly encourage you to use the material in this book in an "à la carte" manner. In other words, pick and choose the questions, activities, Scriptures, age-appropriate ideas, etc. which best fit your family. This book is not intended to serve as a curriculum, requiring compliance with our sequence and plan, but rather as a tool chest from which you can grab what works for you and which can be altered to fit your family situation.

The long and the short of it: Each family night topic presented in this book includes several activities, related Scriptures, and possible discussion items. Do not feel it is necessary to conduct them all in a single family night. You may wish to spread one topic over several weeks using smaller portions of each chapter, depending upon the attention span of the kids and the energy level of the parents. Remember, short and effective is better than long and thorough.

Journaling: Finally, we have provided space with each session for you to capture a record of meaningful comments, funny happenings, and unplanned moments which will inevitably occur during family night. Keep a notebook of these journal entries for future reference. You will treasure this permanent record of the heritage passing process for years to come.

☺ 1: Stewardship

Exploring God's concept of stewardship

Scripture
- Luke 19:12-26—Jesus tells a story about faithful stewards.
- 1 Peter 4:10—Be good servants of God's gifts.

ACTIVITY OVERVIEW		
Activity	Summary	Pre-Session Prep
Activity 1: We Own This?	Identify items family members own.	You'll need a large sheet of poster board or newsprint and colored markers.
Activity 2: Taking Care of Stuff	Create gifts and discover how God asks us to be faithful stewards.	You'll need graham crackers, peanut butter, thin stick pretzels, and small marshmallows.

Main Points:

—God owns everything. He entrusts things to us to manage for Him.

—Being a faithful steward means managing God's things wisely.

LIFE SLOGAN: "God gives things out of His love; things we should take care of."

Make it your own
In the space provided below, outline the flow and add any additional ideas to guide you through the process of conducting this family night.

Prayer & Praise Items
In the space provided below, list any items you wish to pray about or give praise for during this family night session.

Journal
In the space provided below, capture a record of any fun or meaningful things which happened during this family night session.

WARM-UP

Open with Prayer: Begin by having a family member pray, asking God to help everyone in the family understand more about Him through this time. After prayer, review your last lesson by asking these questions:

- **What did we learn about in our last lesson?**
- **What was the Life Slogan?**
- **Have your actions changed because of what we learned? If so, how?** Encourage family members to give specific examples of how they've applied learning from the past week.

Share: Today we're going to discover what the word "stewardship" means, and why God wants us to be faithful stewards of all that He has given us.

ACTIVITY 1: We Own This?

Point: God owns everything. He gives us things to manage according to His plan.

Supplies: You'll need a large sheet of poster board or newsprint and colored markers.

Activity: Place a large sheet of newsprint or poster board on the floor and have everyone sit around it. Set colored markers on the floor within reach of all family members.

Share: Tonight we're going to begin looking at what God wants us to do with the gifts He's given us. Let's begin by each going to our rooms to find one item that we really are glad we own. Choose something that you can carry down to this room.

Age Adjustments

YOUNGER CHILDREN will get more out of this activity if you do a true "inventory" of their belongings rather than a poster board drawing. To do this, go around the house with your children and have them identify items that they own (toys, clothes, etc.). Seeing these items, then talking about how everything we own belongs to God will help younger children understand the significance of "giving it all back to God."

OLDER CHILDREN AND TEENAGERS might enjoy turning the listing activity into a contest. Challenge them to list as many items as they can in a limited time (two or three minutes).

After everyone has returned with their item, ask these questions:
- **Why did you choose that item?** (Because I really like it; because it was the first thing I saw; because it means a lot to me.)
- **What does it feel like to have this item?** (I feel good; it makes me feel special.)

Place the items around the room and have each person begin drawing (or listing) all of the items they're fortunate to own. Parents should list or draw such items as a home, furniture, car, clothes, and so on. Children may draw pictures of toys, clothes, games, and other items.

 After your poster board is packed with words and images, consider these questions:
- **What does this poster board tell us about the stuff we own?** (We have a lot of stuff; we have different kinds of things; our stuff is pretty valuable.)
- **What does it feel like to have all this stuff?** (It feels good; I feel guilty that we have so much; I feel like we don't have enough.)
- **Where did we get all of the things we own?** (From stores; from friends or family members; from God.)

Share: Look at the poster board and everything around us. All that we "own" is truly a gift from God because He actually owns everything. Though we may buy things at a store, or have them given to us as gifts, it is because of God's goodness that we have anything at all. Because these things are a gift from God, God wants us to take care of them and be good "stewards" of all that we have. Being a good steward means using the things God has given us in the best way possible.

ACTIVITY 2: Taking Care of Stuff

Point: Being a faithful steward means managing God's gifts wisely.

 Supplies: You'll need graham crackers, peanut butter, thin stick pretzels, and small marshmallows.

Activity: Make sure family members wash their hands before this activity. Place your supplies on a table and have all family members sit around the table. Explain that each person is going to make an edible creation using food supplies that they can eat at the end of the activity. Help younger children spread the peanut butter and stick marshmallows on the end of the pretzels. Encourage creativity as family members stick the various food items together. [You can also do a similar activity using other supplies, such as pipe cleaners, toothpicks, and gumdrops; the resulting creation won't be edible, of course.]

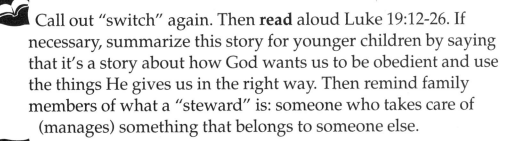

When family members have completed their creations, celebrate each one. Then explain that during the rest of the activity, other family members will be "caretakers" of their snack creations. Tell family members that during the Bible study portion, you'll periodically call out "switch" and family members must carefully take someone else's snack creation and care for it until "switch" is called again. Place a supply of chocolate candies (M&Ms® or something similar) on the table and **share: During the time you're taking care of someone else's snack, think of ways you can make it even better for the person who made it. For example, you may want to stick some of these candies on it using peanut butter. If you do, be careful not to break it.**

 Call out "switch" then have someone **read** aloud 1 Peter 4:10.

 Consider these questions:
- **What does it mean to be a good steward of God's gifts?** (It means we take care of things; it means we need to make sure we don't break things; it means God trusts us with stuff.)
- **How can we be good stewards with the gifts we've been given?** (We can care for things; we can use them wisely; we can share them with others.)

 Call out "switch" again. Then **read** aloud Luke 19:12-26. If necessary, summarize this story for younger children by saying that it's a story about how God wants us to be obedient and use the things He gives us in the right way. Then remind family members of what a "steward" is: someone who takes care of (manages) something that belongs to someone else.

 Call out "switch" again, then consider these questions:
- **Which of the servants were good stewards of what the master had given them?** (The servants who invested the

money; the servants who didn't hide the money.)
- **What did this Bible story tell us about taking care of the things God gives us?** (Taking care of things means using them for God; we don't take care of things by hiding them.)

Share: When we obey God and take care of the things He gives us, we are being good stewards. And if we are good stewards of what we have, God sometimes chooses to trust us with more.

 Have family members retrieve their own snack creations and discuss these questions:
- **What was it like to take care of someone else's snack creation?** (It was scary; it was fun; I worried that I might break it.)
- **How is that like the way we're supposed to take care of the things God gives us?** (We should be careful with the things God's given us; we should do our best in managing what God gives us.)
- **How is your creation different from when you made it?** (It has more candies; it's broken.)
- **How is that like the way we take care of our belongings?** (Sometimes we care for things and they get better; sometimes we don't care for things and they break or don't get used in the right way.) **Share: God has blessed us with many things—clothes, a place to sleep, toys, food, money, and so much more. And God wants us to make wise decisions about how we take care of these things. Let's remember to pray often for help in knowing how to be good stewards of these many great gifts.**

Age Adjustments

OLDER CHILDREN AND TEENAGERS may prefer a more challenging example of "being good stewards." Consider having them create free-standing paper sculptures or other fragile items. This will increase the challenge of caring for the item, and the challenge of finding a way to return it to the original owner showing the effort they have put into it (through coloring or adding items—encourage creativity here).

Have everyone enjoy their snack creation as a celebration of all that God has given you to care for.

WRAP-UP
Gather everyone in a circle and have family members take turns answering this question: **What's one thing you've learned about God today?**

Next, tell kids you've got a new "Life Slogan" you'd like to share with them.

Life Slogan: Today's Life Slogan is this: "God

gives things out of His love; things we should take care of." Have family members repeat the slogan two or three times to help them learn it. Then encourage them to practice saying it during the week so they can talk about it at your next family night session.

Close in Prayer: Allow time for each family member to share prayer concerns and answers to prayer. Then close your time together with prayer for each concern. Thank God for listening to and caring about us.

Remember to record your prayer requests so you can refer to them in the future as you see God answering them.

⊚ 2: Trusting God

Exploring what it means to trust God

Scripture
• Matthew 6:25-34—God takes care of us.
• 1 Kings 17:8-16—God provides for our needs.

ACTIVITY OVERVIEW		
Activity	**Summary**	**Pre-Session Prep**
Activity 1: Who Can You Trust?	Put valuable things in a bag and discuss how difficult it is to trust.	Family members will each need an item they greatly value. You'll also need a Bible.
Activity 2: Change Is Good	Collect loose change from around the house and build up a "trust" fund for emergencies or another important cause.	You'll need a jar or box for holding change, colored paper, tape, markers, and a Bible.

Main Points:

   —Trust isn't easy, but it's important.
   —We can trust that God knows what's best for us.

LIFE SLOGAN: "In God we must place our trust."

Make it your own

In the space provided below, outline the flow and add any additional ideas to guide you through the process of conducting this family night.

Prayer & Praise Items

In the space provided below, list any items you wish to pray about or give praise for during this family night session.

Journal

In the space provided below, capture a record of any fun or meaningful things which happened during this family night session.

 WARM-UP

Open with Prayer: Begin by having a family member pray, asking God to help everyone in the family understand more about Him through this time. After prayer, review your last lesson by asking these questions:

- **What did we learn about in our last lesson?**
- **What was the Life Slogan?**
- **Have your actions changed because of what we learned? If so, how? Encourage family members to give specific examples of how they've applied learning from the past week.**

Share: Today we're going to discover what it means to trust God with our possessions—and how God takes care of us even when it looks like things aren't working out.

ACTIVITY 1: Who Can You Trust?

Point: Trust isn't easy, but it's important.

Supplies: Family members will each need an item they greatly value. You'll also need a Bible.

Activity: As you begin this family night activity, have each family member retrieve an item that they greatly value. Younger children might choose a favorite stuffed animal, a favorite toy, or even a cozy blanket. Older children might choose a video game, a book, or a well-worn shirt. Parents may choose a favorite picture, a wedding album, or a collectible item. Be aware that during this activity, there is a slight possibility that the item might be broken—so choose durable items if possible.

When everyone has returned with an item, discuss these questions:
- **What makes these items valuable to us?** (We like them; they cost a lot of money.)
- **How is that like or unlike the way God feels about us?** (We are important to God; we are worth a lot.)

Have family members place their treasured items together in some high place in your home. For example, you might place the items on a high kitchen shelf, on a fireplace mantel, or in a net or cloth bag suspended from the ceiling.

 Consider these questions:
- **If we were to give these items back to God, would you trust God to care for them? Explain.** (Yes, because God cares for us; I don't know, because I don't know what God would do with them; yes, because God loves us.)
- **Would you trust another family member or a friend with them?** (Probably, because my family likes me and would be careful with this stuff; no, because sometimes my brother breaks things.)
- **Which is easier, trusting God with things, or trusting people?** (Trusting God because He's perfect; trusting people because you can see them.)

Share: Trust isn't easy. As we look at our valued things, we can imagine how we'd feel if they were to be broken, lost, or stolen. And even if we let other people take care of them, these items could be accidentally lost or broken.

 Read aloud Matthew 6:25-34. Then consider these questions:
- **What does this Bible passage tell us about God?** (God will take care of us; we don't need to worry about things because God loves us.)
- **Why can we trust God?** (Because the Bible says so; because God loves us; because God wants the best for us.)

Age Adjustments

YOUNGER CHILDREN may better understand the concept of trust by playing a game. If the weather is pleasant enough, play a simple "water balloon toss" game with your younger children. Before each toss to the child, ask, "Do you trust me to toss this softly?" then toss the balloon softly. Before each toss by the child, ask "Do you trust me to catch this?" Continue until the balloon breaks (preferably on you!). Then discuss why trust is such a difficult thing for humans because we make mistakes. Explain that if God were playing the same game, He would never toss the balloon too hard or miss the toss from the child. In this way, children may discover that they can trust God even more than they trust their parents.

- **What are some things we should trust God with?** (Our family; our problems; our money; our possessions.)

If possible, tell family members you'll leave the valued items where they are for a week or so. Ask family members to remember each time they see the items that they can trust God, even when trusting seems difficult.

ACTIVITY 2: Change Is Good

Point: We can trust that God will take care of us.

 Supplies: You'll need a jar or box for holding change, colored paper, tape, markers, and a Bible.

Activity: Have someone **read** aloud 1 Kings 17:8-16. Then consider these questions:

- **How did God provide for the widow?** (because of her obedience to His word and her willingness to put God first, He provided the basic needs of her family.)
- **What does this tell us about how God will provide for us?** (God will give us what we need; if we ask, God will provide.)

Have family members help decorate a box or jar with colored paper. Then pass the jar around to each family member and ask each person to draw or write on it something that shows how God has provided. For example, someone might draw a picture of a house or a bed, another might write a few words like, "God has given us each other" or "God has given us the Bible to learn from."

Explain that you've just created a "trust fund" box—a place to put change that can be used to help others—and a reminder that we can trust God to care for us even when times are tough.

Then **share: Think about something that you really need right now. It could be a new bicycle, or a pair of clean socks, or even a hug. Don't tell anyone what you're thinking about. We're going to guess what each person is thinking.**

Have volunteers guess what each other person is thinking about. Then **share: We can't always know what each other's needs are, but God always knows what we need—and what's best for us.**

Explain that one way to show that we trust God is to set aside some of our money for people who are less fortunate or who have a great need. You may know of a family in your church or neighborhood who is going through a difficult time. Talk about how giving up some of what we have to help others is a way of saying to God "I trust that You'll take care of me." Then send family members around the house to collect loose change and other money they have that they could put into their new "trust fund."

When family members return, have each drop their change into the "trust fund" box or jar and repeat the following phrase (or something similar) with each dropped handful of coins: **We can save this money for someone who has a great need because we can trust God to take care of us.**

Tell family members that it may be possible in the future that your own family might be the "needy" family who would need the trust fund money. Explain how even this would be a reminder that God takes care of us.

Plan to have a weekly trust fund contribution day where each family member would add to the trust fund box or jar. Over time, you could amass a large sum of money to help another family—or to help your own family out of a tight situation. Take the change to a bank to be changed into bills as a family—and celebrate each dollar as a reminder of how we can trust God to take care of us.

Age Adjustments

OLDER CHILDREN AND TEENAGERS might want to take the discussion of "God's provision" further by discussing such questions as: Does God provide for us in the same miraculous way that He provided food for the widow? Why or why not? How can a sudden job opportunity or an anonymous monetary gift be an example of God's provision? What might God want us to learn from times when we don't have much? Besides financial things, what can we trust God to provide for us?

WRAP-UP

Gather everyone in a circle and have family members take turns answering this question: **What's one thing you've learned about God today?**

Next, tell kids you've got a new "Life Slogan" you'd like to share with them.

Life Slogan: Today's Life Slogan is this: "In God we must place our trust." Have family members repeat the slogan two or three times to help them learn it. Then encourage them to practice saying it during the week so they can talk about it at your next family night session.

Close in Prayer: Allow time for each family member to share prayer concerns and answers to prayer. Then close your time together with prayer for each concern. Thank God for listening to and caring about us.

Remember to record your prayer requests so you can refer to them in the future as you see God answering them.

@ 3: Tithing

Exploring what it means to tithe

Scripture
- Genesis 28:10-22—Jacob promises to give God one-tenth.
- Proverbs 3:9-10—Trust God with your wealth.

ACTIVITY OVERVIEW		
Activity	**Summary**	**Pre-Session Prep**
Activity 1: Tens	Learn what 10 percent looks like and why we should tithe.	Each family member will need to bring ten similar items to the activity. You'll also need a Bible and a box of sweetened cereal.
Activity 2: Celebrate Giving	Enjoy a fun meal to celebrate the joy of giving to God.	You'll need supplies for a celebration dinner. You may want to have some money for each family member too (a regular allowance would be fine).

Main Points:

 —Tithing means giving one-tenth back to God.
 —We give to God because we're thankful.

LIFE SLOGAN: "In order to obey, give one in ten away."

Make it your own
In the space provided below, outline the flow and add any additional ideas to guide you through the process of conducting this family night.

Prayer & Praise Items
In the space provided below, list any items you wish to pray about or give praise for during this family night session.

Journal
In the space provided below, capture a record of any fun or meaningful things which happened during this family night session.

WARM-UP

Open with Prayer: Begin by having a family member pray, asking God to help everyone in the family understand more about Him through this time. After prayer, review your last lesson by asking these questions:

- **What did we learn about in our last lesson?**
- **What was the Life Slogan?**
- **Have your actions changed because of what we learned? If so, how? Encourage family members to give specific examples of how they've applied learning from the past week.**

Share: Today we're going to discover what it means to tithe—and why we give a tithe to God.

ACTIVITY 1: Tens

Point: Tithing means giving one-tenth back to God.

 Supplies: Each family member will need to bring ten similar items to the activity. You'll also need a Bible.

NOTE: If you haven't yet started to tithe, you may want to use this opportunity to begin a commitment along with your children to do just that. It is likely that your children will ask, "Do you tithe?" during this family night, so be prepared to answer honestly and know what plans you have for reaching the goal of giving 10 percent of all you receive.

Activity: Open the activity by having everyone join you in counting to "ten" two or three times. Younger children will enjoy this activity while older children will begin to wonder what tonight's activity will be.

Share: In our first activity tonight we're going to find out what a tithe is. I'll give you a clue: it has something to do with the number ten.

 Ask for volunteers to guess what a tithe is. Some of your older children may already know that it is one-tenth of everything we own and is a gift given back to God. To further illustrate what a tithe is, have someone **read** aloud Genesis 28:10-22.

Then **share: Jacob wanted God to be with him on his journey. As a symbol of his desire to trust God during that journey, Jacob promised to give God one-tenth of all he was given. Giving one-tenth of what we have is called "tithing." "Tithe" is a fancy word for "tenth" and it usually means giving 10 percent of what we have, just as Jacob promised. Let's take a look at what that means.**

Have each family member collect ten similar items from things they own. For example, a young child might bring ten coloring books or building blocks; an elementary-school child might bring ten baseball cards, stuffed animals, or toy "characters"; an older teenager might bring ten T-shirts, magazines, or CDs. Adults might bring ten shoes, computer disks, or books. Have family members lay their ten items on the floor in neat, straight lines.

Consider these questions:

- **What does it feel like to have so many things here on the floor?** (It feels good; I like it; we really are lucky to have this stuff.) Go around and remove one item from each row, setting it in a separate pile nearby. Explain that the single item pile represents 10 percent of all the items. Then consider these questions.
- **How does this small pile compare to the larger rows of stuff?** (It seems really small; it doesn't compare at all; it's just a little bit.)
- **If we consider that God provided all of the things here, how easy or difficult would it be to give this smaller pile back to God?** (It would be easy, because it isn't very much; it would still be difficult because I don't like to give up stuff.)
- **Giving 10 percent (or one out of every ten dollars we have) to God is tithing. Tithing is about more than giving God your money—it involves your time, energy, and talents as well. What does this activity tell us about tithing?** (It should be easy; it isn't very much at all; God deserves more from us than 10 percent.)

Share: The word "tithe" means one-tenth, or one out of every ten dollars. The Bible teaches that we're to tithe by giving one-tenth of all we get back to God. This is usually done by giving to our local church—which can then use the money to help other people to know Christ and to help meet other needs.

Another aspect of tithing that you'll want to teach your family is the concept of "firstfruits." To illustrate this, give each family member ten pieces of sweetened cereal. Ask them to eat nine pieces and save one. Some family members might forget and eat all ten, others might save the smallest or a broken piece as their last piece of cereal.

 Consider these questions:
- **Is it easy to leave one piece of cereal after you've tasted nine? Why or why not?** (No, I want to eat all of it; yes, you asked us to save one; no, I liked it a lot and want one more.)
- **What does this tell us about giving God our tithe after we've spent or used the first nine-tenths of our money or gifts?** (It's not easy to save money to give to God after we've used most of it; it's better to give God our money first.)

Give everyone another ten pieces of cereal and have them choose one piece to give to you as their tithe. Then have everyone enjoy eating the other nine pieces.

 Read aloud Psalm 3:9-10 and discuss:
- **Why should we give to God first?** (Because God asks us to; because God gave everything to us.)
- **What promise does this passage have if we give to God first?** (He will multiply what we receive; we will be blessed; He will care for us.)

Age Adjustments

FOR YOUNGER CHILDREN, the concept of tithing may be difficult to understand. Even the idea of "one out of ten" may be somewhat puzzling to them. To simplify this activity, have young children spread out a bunch of their toys on the floor, then choose one to give to you. Even though you don't focus on the concept of "one out of ten," your young children will begin to understand that it is good to give God some of what you own.

FOR OLDER CHILDREN AND TEENAGERS, take time to talk specifically about their desire to tithe from the earnings they receive through allowances, gifts, and jobs. Your own enthusiasm for and participation in tithing will help them to make a good choice in this matter. If you've had an experience where God has blessed you because of your faithfulness in tithing, be sure to share this with older children.

ACTIVITY 2: Celebrate Giving

Point: We give to God because we're thankful.

 Supplies: You'll need supplies for a celebration dinner. You may want to have some money for each family member too (a regular allowance would be fine).

Activity: Gather decorations, dishes, and food for a fun, celebration meal. You may want to give different responsibilities to each family member to create this celebration. For example, younger children might help set the table, elementary-age children might enjoy decorating the room, and older children and teenagers could help prepare the meal. Choose a menu that your family really enjoys. If you choose to do your family night after dinner, prepare a celebration dessert, instead.

As you prepare the meal or dessert, encourage family members to tell about things God has given them that they're thankful for. Then, when the meal is ready, the table set, and the decorations in place, sit down at the table together.

If you traditionally give out an allowance, do so at the table at this time if possible. Remind children about what it means to tithe and allow them to consider giving 10 percent of their allowance back to God. You may want to provide envelopes for family members to place their tithe.

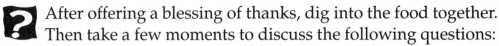 After offering a blessing of thanks, dig into the food together. Then take a few moments to discuss the following questions:
- **Why are we celebrating the idea of giving one-tenth back to God?** (Because we are happy God gave us things in the first place; because it's exciting to give something back to God.)
- **Why do we tithe?** (Because we love God; because God gave to us first.)

Share: It may seem strange to celebrate that we're giving money away, but we're not giving it away foolishly—we're giving it back to the One who gave it to us in the first place. We're celebrating tonight because God has given generously to our family. Our tithes are one way we tell God "thanks for giving us so much."

Make it a tradition to celebrate monthly with a tithe celebration dinner or dessert to remind family members that we tithe because we're thankful and because the Bible teaches us to give one-tenth back to God.

WRAP-UP

Gather everyone in a circle and have family members take turns answering this question: **What's one thing you've learned about God today?**

Next, tell kids you've got a new "Life Slogan" you'd like to share with them.

Life Slogan: Today's Life Slogan is this: "In order to obey, give one in ten away." Have family members repeat the slogan two or three times to help them learn it. Then encourage them to practice saying it during the week so they can talk about it at your next family night session.

Close in Prayer: Allow time for each family member to share prayer concerns and answers to prayer. Then close your time together with prayer for each concern. Thank God for listening to and caring about us.

Remember to record your prayer requests so you can refer to them in the future as you see God answering them.

4: Generously Giving to Others

Exploring what it means to give to others

Scripture
- Luke 10:25-37—Jesus tells the story of the Good Samaritan.
- 2 Corinthians 6–7—If you sow generously, you will reap generously.

ACTIVITY OVERVIEW		
Activity	Summary	Pre-Session Prep
Activity 1: A Giving Attitude	Act out a variation on the "Good Samaritan" story and learn what it means to give joyfully.	You'll need a Bible and soft yarn.
Activity 2: The Helping Box	Gather supplies and deliver them to help someone in need.	You'll need a variety of supplies depending on the activity you choose.

Main Points:

—We can give joyfully to others.

—We can help people when we give generously.

LIFE SLOGAN: "Joy flows like a river from a cheerful giver."

Personal
NOTES

Make it your own
In the space provided below, outline the flow and add any additional ideas to guide you through the process of conducting this family night.

Prayer & Praise Items
In the space provided below, list any items you wish to pray about or give praise for during this family night session.

Journal
In the space provided below, capture a record of any fun or meaningful things which happened during this family night session.

Session Tip

We intentionally have provided more material than we would expect to be used in a single "Family Night" session. You know your family's unique interests and life circumstances best, so feel free to adapt this lesson to meet your family members' needs. Remember, short and simple is better than long and comprehensive.

 ### WARM-UP

Open with Prayer: Begin by having a family member pray, asking God to help everyone in the family understand more about Him through this time. After prayer, review your last lesson by asking these questions:
- **What did we learn about in our last lesson?**
- **What was the Life Slogan?**
- **Have your actions changed because of what we learned? If so, how? Encourage family members to give specific examples of how they've applied learning from the past week.**

Share: Today we're going to explore what it means to have a giving attitude—and why we should be cheerful givers.

ACTIVITY 1: A Giving Attitude

Point: We can give joyfully to others.

Supplies: You'll need a Bible and soft yarn.

Activity: Open the family night by having someone **read** aloud the story of the Good Samaritan in Luke 10:25-37. If your children are younger, you may wish to read the story from a children's Bible. After reading the story, explain that you're now going to act out a similar story to see what it's like to give to someone joyfully.

Have a parent or older child play the part of an "injured person." Softly tie his or her legs to a chair or table to make him or her immobile. Place a cup of water out of reach of the injured person. Then feed your injured person a saltine cracker or two. Have your child (or children) take turns playing the following roles (one child can repeat the activity doing a different role each time):

• Someone who walks by and doesn't even look at the injured person

• Someone who hears the injured person but doesn't want to help
• Someone who helps the injured person, but begrudgingly, or with a bad attitude
• Someone who helps the injured person with a cheerful attitude

Begin the role play by having the injured person call out for a drink of water. Then have your child or children act out the various roles with as much "hamming it up" as they desire. If you like, you may want to switch roles and have other family members play the part of the injured person.

 After this role play, discuss these questions:

• **What was it like to be thirsty and have people ignore you?** (It felt bad; I didn't like it; I wanted someone to stop.)
• **What did it feel like to walk by and not help the injured person?** (It was fun to walk by; it felt bad not to help; I wanted to get him or her a drink of water.)
• **What were you thinking when you finally got to help the person, but with a bad attitude?** (I was glad to help, but sad to be so mean; I would have preferred not to help at all.)
• **How did your feelings change when you helped the injured person with a cheerful attitude?** (It was fun to help; I liked helping with a happy attitude; it made me feel good inside.)

Share: The Bible tells us that we are to be cheerful givers. There are people in need all around us, and God's desire for us is to use the gifts we've been given, whether they be monetary or otherwise, to help those people. Just as it felt good to give water to the injured person, it feels good to give generously to others.

Age Adjustments

FOR YOUNGER CHILDREN, **consider this activity. Choose a toy that your child enjoys and give it to him or her to hold. Then have your family members pass that toy around using their grumpiest faces and attitudes. Young children will enjoy playacting the part of a grumpy person. After a few rounds, have family members pass around that toy using their happiest attitudes. Explain that God wants us to be happy when we give things to others.**

OLDER CHILDREN AND TEENAGERS **can take this discussion a little deeper by considering times when they've received help from people who are happy to help and from people who help begrudgingly, such as when shopping, etc. Ask them to talk about the difference in those two situations and which they preferred. Then encourage your older children to take what they've learned on the receiving end and apply it to the way they give to others.**

ACTIVITY 2: The Helping Box

Point: We can help people when we give generously.

 Supplies: You'll need a variety of supplies depending on the activity you choose.

 Read aloud 2 Corinthians 6–7, then discuss these questions:

- **The Bible tells us to be cheerful givers. What are ways we can give to others?** (We can give them our toys; we can give them our time; we can help them with things.)
- **Who are some people you know who you can help by being a cheerful giver?** (Answers will vary.)

Activity: This family night activity will require a little bit of advance planning. You'll need to be aware of families or individuals who have specific needs that your family might be able to meet. Talk with your pastor or another church leader to discover some of the needs in your community.

The object of the activity is to demonstrate a cheerful giving attitude by putting together a "helping box" of things that can aid another family or person in need. There are many kinds of helping boxes you can create. Here are a few suggestions (some are seasonal):

- The Yard Box. This would include rakes, lawn bags, and other supplies for cleaning leaves from someone's yard.
- The Window Box. This would include window cleaner, paper towels, and other supplies for cleaning windows.
- The Lunch Box. This would include food, utensils, and place settings for making and serving a lunch meal to a person or family.
- The Game Box. This would include game supplies for sharing a game night with a person or family who might need cheering up.

Age Adjustments

FOR YOUNGER CHILDREN, a helping box might have more significance if it included items from their collection of toys, books, and clothes. Help your younger children make good giving decisions by choosing a few items from which they can select one or two to include in the box. It's important for children to feel like they're making their own contributions to the box, rather than you choosing for them. But it could be a daunting and confusing task for children if left alone to come up with those items.

FOR OLDER CHILDREN AND TEENAGERS, consider having them choose a local charity to give to (if they choose to do so cheerfully, of course). Practicing the act of giving money to a reputable charity can have long-term benefits to your older children. Not only will they develop good and generous giving habits, they will begin to see the results of their generosity as they read about what the charitable organizations are doing to help others.

- The Boxes and Cans Box. This would include lots of boxed and canned foods to be given to someone who needs food.
- The Toy Box. This would include lots of toys (in good shape) that could cheer up a family with children who don't have many toys.
- The Everything We Could Fit in It Box. As you might guess, this would include food, toys, tools, and other supplies to share with someone.

You can come up with other helping box ideas too. Encourage your older children to think up a few new ideas. Discuss with your family what kind of helping box you'd like to create to help one of the needs you learned about from your pastor or church leader. Then go around and collect the supplies for the helping box. If your helping box is a "service-oriented" box (like leaf-raking or window-cleaning), set the supplies aside and make a plan for a specific day to take the box to your destination to complete the helping task.

As a sidelight to this activity, consider taking up a collection of "gift" or "charitable donation" funds from family members to give to a local community service organization. This will help your family members begin to see the value of giving generously not only of time and goods, but of money as well.

When your helping box is complete and your plan for delivering it (or doing the service activity) is complete, consider these questions:
- **What does it feel like to put together a box like this?** (It's fun to see what we can find; it's hard work but it feels good; it's a challenge to fill it up.)
- **How can a helping box bring joy to someone else?** (It can help them by giving them something they need; it can make them smile when we clean their windows.)

Share: The Bible says that God loves a cheerful giver. We can help others when we cheerfully deliver this helping box.

WRAP-UP

Gather everyone in a circle and have family members take turns answering this question: **What's one thing you've learned about God today?**

Next, tell kids you've got a new "Life Slogan" you'd like to share with them.

Life Slogan: Today's Life Slogan is this: "Joy flows like a river from a cheerful giver." Have family members repeat the slogan two or three times to help them learn it. Then encourage them to practice saying it during the week so they can talk about it at your next family night session.

Close in Prayer: Allow time for each family member to share prayer concerns and answers to prayer. Then close your time together with prayer for each concern. Thank God for listening to and caring about us.

Remember to record your prayer requests so you can refer to them in the future as you see God answering them.

@ 5: Contentment

Exploring what it means to be content

Scripture
- Matthew 4:1-11—Satan tempts Jesus.
- Matthew 6:33—Seek first the kingdom and His righteousness.
- Hebrews 13:5—Be content, because God will never leave us.

ACTIVITY OVERVIEW		
Activity	Summary	Pre-Session Prep
Activity 1: Identi-Scam	Identify how television commercials manipulate people and lead them to believe they "need" things.	You'll need a television, paper, a pencil, and a Bible.
Activity 2: I'm Happy with My Snack	Learn to be content with the food we're given.	You'll need a package of candies and a Bible.

Main Points:

—We can fight the temptation that makes us want more stuff.

—Contentment is the secret to happiness.

LIFE SLOGAN: "Be content with what God sent."

Make it your own
In the space provided below, outline the flow and add any additional ideas to guide you through the process of conducting this family night.

Prayer & Praise Items
In the space provided below, list any items you wish to pray about or give praise for during this family night session.

Journal
In the space provided below, capture a record of any fun or meaningful things which happened during this family night session.

Session Tip

We intentionally have provided more material than we would expect to be used in a single "Family Night" session. You know your family's unique interests and life circumstances best, so feel free to adapt this lesson to meet your family members' needs. Remember, short and simple is better than long and comprehensive.

WARM-UP

Open with Prayer: Begin by having a family member pray, asking God to help everyone in the family understand more about Him through this time. After prayer, review your last lesson by asking these questions:
- **What did we learn about in our last lesson?**
- **What was the Life Slogan?**
- **Have your actions changed because of what we learned? If so, how? Encourage family members to give specific examples of how they've applied learning from the past week.**

Share: Today we're going to explore what the Bible tells us about being content with the things we have.

ACTIVITY 1: Identi-Scam

Point: We can fight the temptation that makes us want more stuff.

Supplies: You'll need a television, paper, a pencil, and a Bible.

Activity: Gather everyone around the television for this activity. Since you'll be flipping channels in search of commercials, having a remote control handy would be helpful.

Share: We're going to watch television for this family night activity. But we're not going to watch a regular show. We're going to look for commercials. And we're going to play a simple game as we watch the commercials. When you see a commercial, call out what you think the commercial is trying to sell us. For example, if you see a restaurant commercial, you might call out "hamburgers" or "French fries." Call

out your ideas as we flip channels. I'll make a list of those things on a sheet of paper.

NOTE: If you don't have a television or prefer to not use the television for this activity, a similar activity can be done using the advertisements found in magazines. Choose magazines that have ads that would appeal to children and adults so each family member can relate to some of the items that are being sold or prerecord commercials onto a videotape.

Flip channels for a while until you've compiled a large list, then turn off the television. Your list will vary depending on the age of your children, the time of the day, and the channels you flip through. If you have a children's programming channel (like Nickelodeon or the Disney Channel), be sure to flip through that channel so younger children can participate by calling out the names of familiar toys or games advertised.

 Hold up your list and read aloud the items you wrote down. Then discuss these questions:
- **When you see things that interest you in commercials, how do you feel?** (I usually want those things; I think about what it would be like if I had those things; it doesn't affect me.)
- **How do commercials make us want more stuff?** (They show us all the cool new things we haven't seen yet; they make the things look great; they tell us why we need the toys.)
- **How is this goal like a "scam" or a way to trick viewers?** (They try to tell you that you need the stuff; they make you believe you're nobody important if you don't have the items.)
- **What does a commercial do or say to get you to believe you need that item?** (They say "you need this"; they tell you you'll be a better person if you get the item.)

 Read aloud Matthew 4:1-11. Then consider these questions:
- **How is the way Satan tried to trick Jesus like the way the commercials try to trick us?** (Satan tried to tell Jesus He'd be more important if He gave into temptation; Satan tried to bribe Jesus with a promise of more stuff if He gave in.)
- **How did Jesus deal with the temptation to have more "stuff"?** (He reminded Himself, and Satan, of what God says.)
- **What can we learn from this story about the way we should face temptations?** (Remember what God says, not just what we want.)

Read aloud Hebrews 13:5. Then discuss what this passage means and how it applies to the desire for more things that is prompted and fueled by television commercials and other media. Remind everyone that because God has promised never to leave or forget us that our needs will be taken care of. This knowledge can help us overcome the temptation to have "just one more" thing that we really don't need and learn to be happy or content with what we already have.

Ask family members each to complete the following sentence: "One way I can be content or happy with what I have is to . . ." Some responses might include: ". . . play with the toys I already have instead of ask for more" or ". . . fix up our old car instead of spend the money for a new one we don't need."

If you haven't tried a hiatus from television in a while (or at all), this might be an opportune time to suggest it to your family. Seeing all the commercials and their attempts to manipulate us into wanting "more" might help family members accept the idea of a vacation from television. Use the time instead to do more family night activities—or to serve other people using the gifts and material things you already have been given.

ACTIVITY 2: I'm Happy with My Snack

Point: Contentment is the secret to happiness.

 Supplies: You'll need a package of candies and a Bible.

Activity: Set out a bunch of small candies on a table, placing them around the table in separate piles—one pile for each family member. In one pile, place just one or two candies and vary the number in the other piles too. Have family members sit at the table with one of the candy piles in front of them.

Age Adjustments

YOUNGER CHILDREN **may have some difficulty with the concept of temptation. Here's an easy way to help them understand what it means to be tempted. Get a favorite dessert treat or other snack and place it on the dinner table next to their plate before eating dinner. Your younger children will probably feel a strong feeling that they want to eat that item—explain that this is what temptation is: the desire for something that may not be best for us. Once children understand this concept, a return to the television to scan a few commercials will help to solidify the idea that commercials are temptations we need to learn to avoid.**

OLDER CHILDREN AND TEENAGERS **may enjoy another activity to help them see the futility in always wanting more. Hold a dollar bill (or a five-dollar bill, if you so choose) in your fingertips and have your older child place his or her fingers on either side of the middle of the bill. Then ask your child to try and catch the bill with their fingers when you drop it. Repeat this activity a few times. It will be nearly impossible for kids to catch the bill as their response time after you release the bill is too slow to actually pinch the bill. Use this as a springboard to a discussion about how people's desire for more and more stuff is a futile endeavor—much like their attempts to catch the dollar bill.**

Share: We're going to each get to eat the candies in one of these piles at the end of this activity. But before we eat our candies, we're going to play a game to see which pile of candies each person will get.

Read aloud Matthew 6:33, then discuss the following questions. Each time someone answers a question, have everyone get up and move one candy pile to the right. You're bound to get good participation as kids maneuver to get the biggest candy pile.

- **What is the most important thing to seek in life?** (Seek God; seek good for all people; seek love.)
- **What does this passage tell us about our desire for more things?** (We shouldn't look for more stuff; we should be happy with what we have.)
- **What can we learn from this passage to help us face the temptation to get more stuff?** (God will be with us; if we seek God, our needs will be met.)
- **This passage reminds us that if we seek God, He will provide for us. How does God provide for us now?** (God gives us food; God gives us family and friends; God gives us His Bible to learn from.)

Age Adjustments

YOUNGER CHILDREN may have a difficult time understanding why they got fewer candies in this activity if they end up with a smaller pile. Explain that God wants us to be happy with what we have, but that He also wants us to share with one another. At this time, you and other family members may choose to divide up the candies in a more equitable fashion—better yet, increase the pile of those who choose to be content and thankful with their own pile—no grumbling accepted.

When family members don't have anymore answers (or when you call time), explain that they can now eat the candies that are in front of them. Remind everyone that God calls us to be happy with what we have. Ask everyone to put on their biggest smiles to enjoy the candies.

Share: The secret to being happy is to learn to be content. We can do this by obeying God, trusting that He will provide, and serving Him. God has promised to take care of us, so we can learn to be happy with what we have—whether we have a lot (like the people who got the biggest candy piles) or a little (like the people with the smaller candy piles).

WRAP-UP
Gather everyone in a circle and have family members take turns answering this question: **What's one thing you've learned about God today?**

Next, tell kids you've got a new "Life Slogan" you'd like to share with them.

Life Slogan: Today's Life Slogan is this: "Be content with what God sent." Have family members repeat the slogan two or three times to help them learn it. Then encourage them to practice saying it during the week so they can talk about it at your next family night session.

Close in Prayer: Allow time for each family member to share prayer concerns and answers to prayer. Then close your time together with prayer for each concern. Thank God for listening to and caring about us.

Remember to record your prayer requests so you can refer to them in the future as you see God answering them.

☉ 6: Honesty

Exploring what it means to speak and act in truth

Scripture
- Acts 5:1-11—Ananias and Sapphira lie to God.
- Proverbs 10:9; 11:3; 12:5; 14:2; 28:13—(Proverbs about honesty).

ACTIVITY OVERVIEW		
Activity	Summary	Pre-Session Prep
Activity 1: Pizza Box Parable	Experience what it feels like to be lied to.	You'll need two pizza boxes—one empty and one with a fresh, hot pizza—and a Bible.
Activity 2: No, Honestly!	Lie or tell the truth about holding coins.	You'll need a bunch of coins and a Bible.

Main Points:

—Lying has consequences and can hurt people.

—Honesty means being sure we tell the truth and are fair.

LIFE SLOGAN: "Telling the truth is not so odd; it shows that we trust in God."

Personal
NOTES

Make it your own
In the space provided below, outline the flow and add any additional ideas to guide you through the process of conducting this family night.

Prayer & Praise Items
In the space provided below, list any items you wish to pray about or give praise for during this family night session.

Journal
In the space provided below, capture a record of any fun or meaningful things which happened during this family night session.

Session Tip

We intentionally have provided more material than we would expect to be used in a single "Family Night" session. You know your family's unique interests and life circumstances best, so feel free to adapt this lesson to meet your family members' needs. Remember, short and simple is better than long and comprehensive.

WARM-UP

Open with Prayer: Begin by having a family member pray, asking God to help everyone in the family understand more about Him through this time. After prayer, review your last lesson by asking these questions:

- What did we learn about in our last lesson?
- What was the Life Slogan?
- Have your actions changed because of what we learned? If so, how? Encourage family members to give specific examples of how they've applied learning from the past week.

Share: Today we're going to examine what it means to be honest and why God wants us to be honest in all we say and do.

ACTIVITY 1: Pizza Box Parable

Point: Lying has consequences and can hurt people.

Supplies: You'll need two pizza boxes—one empty and one with a fresh, hot pizza—and a Bible.

Activity: Make plans for a "pizza picnic party" in front of the television or a favorite family video. (We suggest videos such as "McGee and Me: The Big Lie" or the Veggie Tales video, "The Fib from Outer Space." Both deal with honesty.) For this activity to work, you'll need to secretly collect an empty pizza box along with  the real pizza. When you're ready to start the pizza picnic party, enter the room with the empty box and begin your party. Begin with prayer, then have children open the box. After the quizzical looks and complaints die down, admit you lied.

 Consider these questions:
- **What did you feel when you learned that I lied?** (Upset; angry; confused.)
- **How is that like the way other people feel when you lie?** (It's similar; people get angry with me when I don't tell the truth.)
- **What were the consequences of my lie?** (We don't have any food; we're unhappy; people are hurt.)

Read aloud or summarize the story of Ananias and Sapphira found in Acts 5:1-11. Use this Bible story to help children understand that lies have consequences and can hurt people. Then admit to your children that the empty pizza box was just a way to get them thinking about lies. Bring out the real pizza and celebrate the importance of honesty together with your pizza picnic party.

ACTIVITY 2: No, Honestly!

Point: Honesty means being sure we tell the truth and are fair.

Supplies: You'll need a bunch of coins and a Bible.

Age Adjustments

FOR OLDER CHILDREN AND TEENAGERS, use this activity as an opportunity for family members (that means you too) to "come clean" about lies that have been plaguing them. While this could become an intense emotional time if hurtful lies are revealed, it may be the beginning of a new, honest relationship between you and your children. If all family members report they have been totally truthful, celebrate the honesty in your family with a great big group hug. If you uncover a lie, thank the child for being honest; spend time in prayer; and form a group hug to acknowledge the importance of being honest with one another. Wait until morning to decide how to respond to any lies that might warrant some kind of consequence.

Activity: Give each family member two coins. Then explain that you're going to play a game called "No, honestly!" Have everyone stand in a circle.

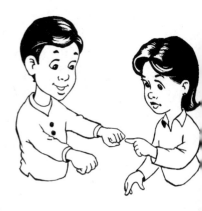

Share: Here's how we play. Secretly put one, two, or no coins in one hand and close your fist around them. Then hold your closed fist out toward someone else in our family. Then tell that person how many coins are in your hand (without opening your hand). You can tell the truth, or you can lie and tell that person you have one when you have two, two when

you have none, and so on. If the person you're telling believes you, you don't have to open your hand. If the person you're telling doesn't believe you, he or she must say "Really?" Then you must show that person what's in your hand.

 Go around the circle until each person has played at least once. Then discuss the following questions:

- **What was it like to be caught telling a lie?** (I didn't like it; I was surprised people challenged me; I never told a lie.)
- **Was it easy to lie or fool people? Why or why not?** (Yes, because people trusted me; no, because people kept challenging me.)
- **Is it easy to lie in real life? Explain.** (Sometimes, because people think I always tell the truth; no, because I always get caught; yes, people do it all the time at school.)
- **How is this game like what happens in real life?** (Sometimes I get caught lying; sometimes I lie and get away with it; I don't like what it feels like to lie.)

Share: In this game, we decided it was OK to lie. But just as you may have felt bad about lying in this game, it feels bad to lie in real life.

Age Adjustments

YOUNGER CHILDREN may choose to always tell the truth in the coin activity. If you sense that they're always telling the truth (or if it's proven during the activity), congratulate them on being honest. Point out to all family members how we get "better" at deception as we get older, which is not a good tendency.

OLDER CHILDREN AND TEENAGERS can take this activity further by discussing each of the Proverbs in greater detail and talking about how those Proverbs apply today to their lives. For example, a discussion of Proverbs 10:9 might lead children and teenagers to talk about friends at school who are caught in lies and the consequences they must face.

 Read aloud a selection of Proverbs from the following list: Proverbs 10:9; 11:3; 12:5; 14:2; 28:13.

 Then discuss the following questions:
- **Why do you think there are so many Bible passages about being honest?** (Because lying is wrong; God wants us to tell the truth.)
- **What happens when we lie or are dishonest?** (We disobey God; we hurt people; we feel bad.)

Share: Being honest means bringing out the truth in what we do and say. Everything works better when we tell the truth: families; finances; friendships; and everything else. When we choose honesty, we show that we trust God. Being honest also means being fair. If we owe

someone five dollars, we should pay them five dollars. Giving them less would be unfair—and dishonest. And when we're dishonest to other people, we're also dishonest to God.

WRAP-UP

Gather everyone in a circle and have family members take turns answering this question: **What's one thing you've learned about God today?**

Next, tell kids you've got a new "Life Slogan" you'd like to share with them.

Life Slogan: Today's Life Slogan is this: "Telling the truth is not so odd; it shows that we trust in God." Have family members repeat the slogan two or three times to help them learn it. Then encourage them to practice saying it during the week so they can talk about it at your next family night session.

Close in Prayer: Allow time for each family member to share prayer concerns and answers to prayer. Then close your time together with prayer for each concern. Thank God for listening to and caring about us.

Remember to record your prayer requests so you can refer to them in the future as you see God answering them.

@ 7: Diligence

Exploring what it means to work hard

Scripture
- Genesis 39–41—Joseph shows he is diligent.
- Colossians 3:23-24—Whatever you do, do it as unto the Lord.

ACTIVITY OVERVIEW		
Activity	Summary	Pre-Session Prep
Activity 1: Giving Your Best	Discover the difference between doing something "just to get by" and doing something with excellence.	You'll need children's blocks or a large supply of cardboard boxes.
Activity 2: Workin' Hard	Brainstorm jobs to do around the house—then do them.	You'll need a Bible, paper, and a pencil. Other supplies needed will vary depending on the jobs chosen.

Main Points:

—Being diligent means working hard.

—God wants our best effort in all we do.

LIFE SLOGAN: "In all we do, we must give our all."

Make it your own

In the space provided below, outline the flow and add any additional ideas to guide you through the process of conducting this family night.

Prayer & Praise Items

In the space provided below, list any items you wish to pray about or give praise for during this family night session.

Journal

In the space provided below, capture a record of any fun or meaningful things which happened during this family night session.

Session Tip

We intentionally have provided more material than we would expect to be used in a single "Family Night" session. You know your family's unique interests and life circumstances best, so feel free to adapt this lesson to meet your family members' needs. Remember, short and simple is better than long and comprehensive.

WARM-UP

Open with Prayer: Begin by having a family member pray, asking God to help everyone in the family understand more about Him through this time. After prayer, review your last lesson by asking these questions:

- What did we learn about in our last lesson?
- What was the Life Slogan?
- Have your actions changed because of what we learned? If so, how? Encourage family members to give specific examples of how they've applied learning from the past week.

Share: Today we're going to explore what the word "diligence" means and why we should word hard to reach our goals and the goals God has for us.

ACTIVITY 1: Giving Your Best

Point: God wants our best effort in all we do.

Supplies: You'll need children's blocks or a large supply of cardboard boxes.

Activity: Set the children's blocks (or boxes) in the middle of the room on the floor. Have everyone sit around the blocks. Then ask family members to take turns creating the tallest tower possible using the blocks. Alternately encourage family members to rush to build their towers; take their time; do a sloppy tower; do a neat and careful tower; and so on. Give everyone at least one attempt at building a tower.

? Then consider these questions:

- **What was it like to build a sloppy or quick tower?** (The tower kept falling down; it wasn't very stable; I didn't like racing around.)
- **How did you feel when you created a neat, carefully built tower?** (Like I'd done something good; it felt great to see such a nice tower.)
- **Which kind of tower would you build if you were building it for God?** (The nicest, prettiest tower; I'd spend time to do it right; I'd still want to do one quickly.)

Age Adjustments

FOR YOUNGER CHILDREN, the "doing your best" concept can be hammered home as they learn to write their names or draw pictures. Ask your younger children to draw messy letters or pictures and then neat, careful letters or pictures. Use this illustration to teach them that God wants us to do our best—like the neat, careful letters and pictures—in all we do.

OLDER CHILDREN AND TEENAGERS will understand the concept of excellence in many different ways. If your children enjoy video games, have them compare average games with excellent ones and identify what makes some better than others. Help them understand that diligence is likely what made the one game better. A similar discussion can be done using other objects from an older child or teenager's world, such as clothes; make-up; sports equipment or teams; movies; music; and much more.

📖 Read aloud Colossians 3:23-24. Then **share: The Bible tells us that we're to do everything as if unto God. That means when we brush our teeth we should do our best as if we were doing it for God. It means that when we pick up our rooms they should be as neat as possible as if we're doing it for God. How does this idea affect other things that we do?** (We need to work harder at school; we should work harder at our chores; we need to do a better job of taking care of our money.)

Consider creating a "job board" listing the kinds of jobs family members could do around the house. Include things that aren't already part of regular chores and assign a monetary value to each job (to be paid upon completion). You can use the ideas from the next activity and add other jobs as you think of them. They should be expected to complete the jobs with excellence and should be inspected before payment is made.

ACTIVITY 2: Workin' Hard

Point: Being diligent means working hard and working well.

 Supplies: You'll need a Bible, paper, and a pencil. Other supplies needed will vary depending on the jobs chosen.

Activity: Begin the activity by having family members list as many "around-the-house" jobs as they can. This could include current chores such as taking out the trash, making beds, cleaning rooms, and doing the dishes as well as occasional jobs they may or may not do including cleaning the garage, washing the windows, dusting the furniture, and so on. Write this list on a sheet of paper.

Then go through the items on the list with your children and assign a value to each one. For example, washing the car might be worth $5 while picking up the basement might be worth $2. Some jobs (like regular chores) might be worth no money at all (since they may be included in a child's allowance already). The value of each job should be dependent on the amount of work required to complete it. Longer, more difficult jobs should be worth more than shorter, easier jobs.

NOTE: If you prefer not to do this activity with money, consider using a "candy value" for each item on the list. In this case, washing the car might be worth five candy bars or a box of donuts while picking up the basement might be worth one pack of Life Savers.

After each item has been assigned a value, have each family member choose one job they can complete during the next half hour or so. Help younger children choose jobs they can do well. After jobs are chosen and approved (you need to make sure they're possible with the time and supplies you have, and challenging enough to make everyone work hard), determine together how you'll know if the job is done right. Write a brief description of this next to the job listing so all family members understand the expectation for the job.

Then have family members go to do their various jobs. If someone finishes a job, have all family members check the quality of the job against the expectations written on the job list. If the job passes inspection, award that person the appropriate pay (or food reward if you choose that option). If not, send that person back to the job to complete it according to the expectations.

You may need to help younger children with their jobs, but be sure to let them work as hard as they can to complete them on their own. The object of this activity is to have family members realize what it means to work hard for their keep.

After all jobs are completed, form a circle and discuss:

- **What was it like to do your job?** (It was fun, but a lot of work; it took more time than I thought; I didn't enjoy it at all.)
- **What did it feel like to get your payment or reward after you had completed your job?** (I felt better about all the hard work I'd done; it didn't seem like enough; I felt good about myself.)

Summarize the story of Joseph from Genesis 39–41. If you have time, you might want to read the entire passage, but a summary might include the following:

- Joseph worked hard even when unjustly sold as a slave since he worked like he was working for God, not for people.
- Because Joseph worked for God, he worked diligently and did his job with excellence. God was able to bless him and reward him.
- Joseph's masters saw that Joseph was not only a great worker, but that everything went well when he was in charge. As a result they promoted him.

 After your discussion, ask:

- **What does this story tell us about working hard?** (God wants us to work hard; if you work hard, people will notice; working hard gives rewards.)
- **What are ways we can be diligent like Joseph?** (Work harder on homework; clean my room more often; spend more time reading the Bible.)

Age Adjustments

YOUNGER CHILDREN will need a few jobs catered to their ability level. For example, something like picking up a room might be a regular unpaid chore for an older child, but it could be a job with pay for a younger child. Other ideas for younger children might include dusting the furniture, cleaning the baseboards, helping to gather or fold the laundry.

Share: Being diligent means working hard. We learn from Joseph's story that hard work usually pays off with rewards. But sometimes those rewards aren't as obvious as a promotion or more money. But when we do everything as if working for God, our best reward is our obedience to Him and His promise to bless us.

WRAP-UP

Gather everyone in a circle and have family members take turns answering this question: **What's one thing you've learned about God today?**

Next, tell kids you've got a new "Life Slogan" you'd like to share with them.

Life Slogan: Today's Life Slogan is this: "In all we do, we must give our all." Have family members repeat the slogan two or three times to help them learn it. Then encourage them to practice saying it during the week so they can talk about it at your next family night session.

 **Close in Prayer:** Allow time for each family member to share prayer concerns and answers to prayer. Then close your time together with prayer for each concern. Thank God for listening to and caring about us.

Remember to record your prayer requests so you can refer to them in the future as you see God answering them.

⊚ 8: Planning for the Future

Exploring how to set goals and make plans

Scripture
• Psalm 139:1-18—God knows us and has a plan for us.
• Proverbs 3:5-6—Trust God with all your heart.

ACTIVITY OVERVIEW		
Activity	Summary	Pre-Session Prep
Activity 1: Steps	Play a game to discover the importance of planning.	You'll need paper, scissors, pencils, a treat, and a Bible.
Activity 2: Map Makers	Create maps illustrating where you want to be in the future.	You'll need paper and pencils, markers, or crayons.

Main Points:

—Meeting goals requires smart planning.

—All our plans should match God's plans for us.

LIFE SLOGAN: "If we fail to plan, we plan to fail."

Make it your own

In the space provided below, outline the flow and add any additional ideas to guide you through the process of conducting this family night.

Prayer & Praise Items

In the space provided below, list any items you wish to pray about or give praise for during this family night session.

Journal

In the space provided below, capture a record of any fun or meaningful things which happened during this family night session.

WARM-UP

Open with Prayer: Begin by having a family member pray, asking God to help everyone in the family understand more about Him through this time. After prayer, review your last lesson by asking these questions:

- **What did we learn about in our last lesson?**
- **What was the Life Slogan?**
- **Have your actions changed because of what we learned? If so, how? Encourage family members to give specific examples of how they've applied learning from the past week.**

Share: Today we're going to discover the importance of planning for our future.

ACTIVITY 1: Steps

Point: Meeting goals requires smart planning.

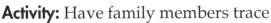

Supplies: You'll need paper, scissors, pencils, a treat, and a Bible.

Activity: Have family members trace their feet onto six sheets of paper and then cut out the feet. You'll need to help trace younger children's feet and help them with the scissors. When each person has six paper feet, line up at one end of a room. Place a sheet of paper with the word "goal" written on it on the floor about five feet away. Then explain the object of this game: for family members to place their feet on the floor in such a way that they can reach the goal and touch it. Tell everyone that they may only step on their paper feet as they try to reach the goal. Family members will enjoy this activity as they plan and place their paper feet, then attempt to walk over and touch the goal paper without falling.

After one round, move the goal paper farther back and repeat the activity. Do this a few times until it becomes difficult (or even impossible) to reach the goal with just six paper feet.

Then have everyone gather up their paper feet and sit in a circle. Discuss the following questions:

• **What was it like to try and reach the goal each time?** (It was fun; I had to plan carefully where to put the feet; I couldn't reach it very easily.)

• **What does this activity tell us about the importance of careful planning?** (If we fail to plan, we plan to fail.)

Play the game again, but this time set up two goals—one on each side of the room. Make sure family members can't easily reach both goals with their six paper feet. Place a treat (like a candy bar, a donut, or a snack-size bag of chips) near the closer of the goals. At the other goal, place a sign that reads "You can have twice as much of the treat if you visit me—but you'll have to wait until tomorrow to receive your treat."

Allow family members to attempt to reach either (or both) goals using their paper feet. After their attempts, discuss these questions:

• **Was it difficult to choose which goal to go for? Why or why not?** (Yes, I wanted more of the treat, but I was also hungry; no, I knew I wanted the treat right away; no, I tried to reach both goals.)

• **What does this activity tell us about our goals?** (Sometimes you have to be patient to get what you want; if you try to do too much at once, sometimes you end up with nothing.)

Have someone **read** aloud Proverbs 3:5-6. Then **share: We discovered in this game that it's important to plan in order to reach our goals. This Bible passage also tells us that we should look to God for guidance on how we should plan. God can help us make good choices as**

Age Adjustments

YOUNGER CHILDREN may have a difficult time understanding the concept of financial planning for the future. However, you can help them by talking about things that they already plan for, such as getting ready for bed. As you prepare a young child for bed, show him or her what happens when you don't plan by forgetting to turn down the bed, forgetting to get the bedtime clothes ready, or forgetting to take the cap off the toothpaste tube. Younger children can then begin to understand that planning means getting things ready for what you want to do later.

OLDER CHILDREN AND TEENAGERS can explore the idea of planning for future educational opportunities and career choices. Have Older Children and Teenagers list a few "life goals" on a sheet of paper, then list as many steps as possible that they might have to take to reach those goals. Not only will this activity help them think about what they want to do in the future, it will be good practice for the kind of financial planning they'll need to do in order to reach those goals.

we think about the future. It is especially important to make good plans for our finances or our money.

ACTIVITY 2: Map Makers

Point: All our plans should match God's plans for us.

> **Supplies:** You'll need paper and pencils, markers, or crayons.

 Activity: Read aloud Psalm 139:1-18, then reread Psalm 139:16.

Share: God has a plan for each of us. While we may not know what that plan is today, we can begin to prepare for the future so that we may someday fulfill the plans God has for us. When we plan, we are being good stewards of what God gives us. (Remind family members what it means to be a good steward by referring them to the family night activities they did on stewardship—see pages 15–21.)

Give each family member a sheet of paper and a pencil or other writing utensil. Younger children might enjoy using crayons or markers. Ask each person to think about one place they'd like to visit anywhere in the world. Younger children might come up with such simple choices as "McDonald's" or "the playground," while older children will likely come up with more exotic locations.

Have family members write their location at the top of their paper (or draw a symbol representing that location). Then ask each person to think of all the steps it would take to get to that goal. You'll want to help younger children by asking them such questions as: "What do we need to do before we go to this place?" and "What will we need when we get there?"

Some of the steps older children might list would include: cost of the trip; supplies needed; how they would get the money; and other things. It would be helpful to have a travel section from a local newspaper to get a general idea about airfare and other travel costs. Or you can simply come up with an acceptable figure together.

When all the steps are listed, have each family member share their dream location and their steps for getting there. Ask everyone to add other steps they think of to family members' presentations.

 Then consider these questions:
- **What were your first thoughts when I asked you to think of a place you'd like to go?** (I was excited; I knew just where

I'd like to go; I couldn't think of any place I'd want to go.)
- **How is that like the way you feel as you think about where God may want you to go in the future?** (I'm excited about what God will want me to do; it's a bit scary to think about where God wants me to go.)
- **What surprised you as you listed the steps to get to your location?** (I didn't think it would take so many steps; I wished it wouldn't be so expensive; I thought it would be easier to get there.)
- **What does this activity tell you about the role of money in planning?** (We need to save up for things we want; if we don't have the money we need, we can't reach our goals.)
- **How is this type of plan similar to plans we might make for other things in the future?** (We need to make plans to pay for college; we need to make plans when we go on a long trip; we need to make plans for the day when we don't have a job.)

Share: A financial plan helps us to reach different goals in our lives such as buying a toy; going on a vacation; buying a house; paying for a wedding; getting into college; and preparing for retirement. But no financial goal would be complete if we left God out of the equation.

There are three elements we must think about as we plan for the future: God has a plan for us; God has given us unique gifts that match His plan for us; and God will guide and direct us when we pray for wisdom and direction. It's important that we seek to match our plans to God's plans for us, so that we might get to those goals in our relationships, finances, career, and all of life.

WRAP-UP

Gather everyone in a circle and have family members take turns answering this question: **What's one thing you've learned about God today?**

Next, tell kids you've got a new "Life Slogan" you'd like to share with them.

Life Slogan: Today's Life Slogan is this: "If we fail to plan, we plan to fail." Have family members repeat the slogan two or three times to help them learn it. Then encourage them to practice saying it during the week so they can talk about it at your next family night session.

Close in Prayer: Allow time for each family member to share prayer concerns and answers to prayer. Then close your time together with prayer for each concern. Thank God for listening to and caring about us.

Remember to record your prayer requests so you can refer to them in the future as you see God answering them.

@ 9: Budgeting

Exploring how to create a budget

Scripture
• Judges 6–7—God helps Gideon budget the men needed in his army.
• Luke 14:28-35—Counting the cost.

ACTIVITY OVERVIEW		
Activity	Summary	Pre-Session Prep
Activity 1: Timetable	Create illustrations of how they use or would like to use their time.	You'll need a table, large sheets of paper, and markers or crayons.
Activity 2: Priorities	Create a financial budget and discover how to determine budgeting priorities.	You'll need a supply of beans (anything from jelly beans to dry beans will do), paper, pencils, and a Bible.

Main Points:

— Budgeting means making a plan for using our money.
— For a budget to work, the money that comes in has to equal the money that goes out.

LIFE SLOGAN: "A wise steward knows where his money goes."

Make it your own

In the space provided below, outline the flow and add any additional ideas to guide you through the process of conducting this family night.

Prayer & Praise Items

In the space provided below, list any items you wish to pray about or give praise for during this family night session.

Journal

In the space provided below, capture a record of any fun or meaningful things which happened during this family night session.

Session Tip

We intentionally have provided more material than we would expect to be used in a single "Family Night" session. You know your family's unique interests and life circumstances best, so feel free to adapt this lesson to meet your family members' needs. Remember, short and simple is better than long and comprehensive.

WARM-UP

Open with Prayer: Begin by having a family member pray, asking God to help everyone in the family understand more about Him through this time. After prayer, review your last lesson by asking these questions:

- **What did we learn about in our last lesson?**
- **What was the Life Slogan?**
- **Have your actions changed because of what we learned? If so, how? Encourage family members to give specific examples of how they've applied learning from the past week.**

Share: Today we're going to find out what a budget is and why it's important to stick to a budget.

ACTIVITY 1: Timetable

Point: Budgeting means making a plan for using our money (Judges 6–7).

Supplies: You'll need a table, large sheets of paper, and markers or crayons.

Activity: Have everyone sit around a table. Give each person a sheet of paper and a marker or crayon. Then have each person draw a large circle on his or her paper. Explain that the circle represents one typical weekday—a 24-hour period. Then have family members divide their circle into pie slices and mark them to indicate how each hour of the day is currently being spent. Younger children will need some help in creating their chart and determining how they spend their time. Some categories to consider would include: sleeping; eating; school; studying; praying; playing with friends;

reading; doing chores; watching television; and so on.

 When the charts are complete, have each person show the rest of the family what each pie slice represents. Then consider the following questions:

- **What does your pie chart tell you about how you spend your time?** (I didn't know I spent so much time sleeping; I learned that I don't spend enough time on homework; I spend too much time watching television.)
- **What things would you change about the way you spend your time?** (Answers will vary.)

Have family members turn over their papers and draw another circle. Have them divide the circle into pie slices representing how they'd like to spend their 24 hours. For some family members, this may not look much different than their other chart. For others, there may be many changes.

 When these charts are complete, have each person share them with the whole family. Then consider these questions:

- **How easy or difficult was it to find a way to use the time?** (I ran out of hours pretty quickly; I didn't know how to fit everything in; it was easy because it's similar to the way I spend my time now.)

Share: What we just did was create a "time budget." If we had all the time in the world, we wouldn't need to be so careful with our time because we could always find more. We *don't* have all the time in the world, though, so we need to plan how to use our time so we can get everything done that we need to do, as well as things we want to do.

In the same way, we all need a "money budget" because we only have so much money. That's why you kids need to develop the skills now, that you'll use more and more as you get older, about spending money wisely.

ACTIVITY 2: Priorities

Point: For a budget to work, the money that comes in has to equal the money that goes out (Luke 14:28-35).

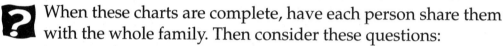 **Supplies:** You'll need a supply of beans (anything from jelly beans to dry beans will do), paper, pencils, and a Bible.

Activity: If you just completed the "Timetable" activity, continue on with the discussion that follows. If you skipped that activity or did it on a previous night, take a moment to talk about a time budget and how it works. You can refer to the previous activity for ideas on what to say.

 Consider these questions:
- **What would happen if you didn't budget enough time for sleep or food?** (We'd be tired; we wouldn't be awake enough to do other things; we'd always be hungry.)

Share: When we make a time budget, we need to make sure important things like sleeping and eating are taken care of first—for without them, we wouldn't be able to do anything else. Sometimes it's difficult to find time for all the things we'd want to do. This is also true for a monetary budget. Each of us only has a limited income—or amount of money we get. If we don't carefully plan how we'll use that money, we'll run out before important things are taken care of. Let's take a look at how that works.

Distribute a supply of dry beans to each family member. The amount distributed will depend on the amount of income each family member has. It will also depend on the value given to each bean. For example, if you have a child who earns $20 a week, that child might get twenty beans, with each bean representing one dollar. A younger child who earns $2.50 a week might only get ten beans, with each representing a quarter. If at all possible, make sure the number of beans is divisible by ten—so a tithe can easily be calculated during the activity.

Age Adjustments

FOR OLDER CHILDREN AND TEENAGERS, consider subdividing the budget on the grid into more detailed categories. You'll find a plan for how to do this in the books *Money Matters for Kids* (ages 8–12) and *Money Matters for Teens* (ages 12–16) (Moody Press).

Have family members draw four boxes on a sheet of paper and list one of the following categories in each box: tithe; short-term savings (things that might take a few weeks or more to save for); long-term savings (money to save for college or an automobile; or money for large purchases such as a bicycle or computer); and spending. Younger children might want to draw a picture to represent each category. Explain each of the categories in terms each child will understand. For example, younger children will understand giving money to church and spending it, but will need help thinking about saving money for things like a new game (short-term savings) or saving for a new bicycle (long-term savings).

Then explain the following suggested formula for budgeting and have family members move the appropriate number of beans into each of the corresponding boxes based on the percentages: tithe—10 percent; short-term savings—25 percent; long-term savings—25 percent; spending—40 percent. It's OK to round up or down the number of beans in each grid space.

 Consider these questions:
- **As you look at this budget, what thoughts do you have?** (I don't have much money to spend; this isn't easy to do; why do I have to save so much money?)
- **How realistic is it to use your money in this way?** (It can be done; I'd have to change how I use it now.)
- **What would be the hardest thing about following a budget like this?** (Saving money instead of spending it; knowing what to save up for; tithing.)

Have family members move all of their beans into the "spending" box. Have volunteers share what the consequences would be if they spent all of their money and didn't save or tithe any. Then have everyone move all of their beans into the long-term savings box. Discuss why this might be a foolish thing to do.

 Consider these questions:
- **Prioritizing means choosing to take care of the most important things first. Why is it important to prioritize when we budget?** (So we don't forget things we have to spend money on; so we don't run out of money.)
- **What are the most important things you should budget your money for?** (Giving to the church; saving for when we really need it; saving for big purchases.)

 Read or summarize the story of Gideon and God's assistance with his "budget" of soldiers (see Judges 7:7) found in Judges 6–7. Help your family members see how God gave Gideon good budgeting advice so he wouldn't use too many soldiers to fight a battle. Compare that decision to the budgeting decisions you and your family members have made (both good and bad).

Ask family members to think and pray about their budgets and how they would like to use their money. Encourage them to follow the suggested distribution of income, but allow them to make their own decisions. Sometimes, it takes a few months of "everything in

the spending box" for a child to realize that the bicycle they really want is still out of reach. At this point, some children will make the adjustment and begin saving on their own.

WRAP-UP

Gather everyone in a circle and have family members take turns answering this question: **What's one thing you've learned about God today?**

Next, tell kids you've got a new "Life Slogan" you'd like to share with them.

Life Slogan: Today's Life Slogan is this: "A wise steward knows where his money goes." Have family members repeat the slogan two or three times to help them learn it. Then encourage them to practice saying it during the week so they can talk about it at your next family night session.

Close in Prayer: Allow time for each family member to share prayer concerns and answers to prayer. Then close your time together with prayer for each concern. Thank God for listening to and caring about us.

Remember to record your prayer requests so you can refer to them in the future as you see God answering them.

⊙ 10: Saving & Investing

Exploring how to prepare for the future through saving

Scripture
- Genesis 41—Joseph's "savings" plan is outlined.
- Proverbs 21:20—Wise people save for times of need.
- Matthew 6:19-21—Don't store up treasures; serve God first.

ACTIVITY OVERVIEW		
Activity	Summary	Pre-Session Prep
Activity 1: Time Machine	Discover how interest works.	You'll need two and a half dollars for each family member and a Bible.
Activity 2: Time Flies	Learn the value of patience and diligence in saving.	You'll need supplies for making cookies and a Bible.

Main Points:

—Investing and saving adds value to money.

—Adding value to money through saving takes time.

LIFE SLOGAN: "Put money away for another day."

Make it your own

In the space provided below, outline the flow and add any additional ideas to guide you through the process of conducting this family night.

Prayer & Praise Items

In the space provided below, list any items you wish to pray about or give praise for during this family night session.

Journal

In the space provided below, capture a record of any fun or meaningful things which happened during this family night session.

Session Tip

We intentionally have provided more material than we would expect to be used in a single "Family Night" session. You know your family's unique interests and life circumstances best, so feel free to adapt this lesson to meet your family members' needs. Remember, short and simple is better than long and comprehensive.

 WARM-UP

Open with Prayer: Begin by having a family member pray, asking God to help everyone in the family understand more about Him through this time. After prayer, review your last lesson by asking these questions:

- What did we learn about in our last lesson?
- What was the Life Slogan?
- Have your actions changed because of what we learned? If so, how? Encourage family members to give specific examples of how they've applied learning from the past week.

Share: Today we're going to explore what saving and investing is all about and why saving is a good thing to do with our money.

ACTIVITY 1: Time Machine

Point: Investing and saving adds value to money.

Supplies: You'll need two and a half dollars for each family member.

Activity: Give each family member one dollar and have them place the money in front of them on a table or on the floor. **Read** aloud Proverbs 21:20 and explain that you're going to do an activity that illustrates why it can be a good thing to save money instead of spending it all right away. Tell family members that you're going to take them on an imaginary "journey through time" ten years into the future.

Have family members stand, close their eyes, and begin spinning in place for their "traveling" time. While they do this, secretly add another dollar and a half to each dollar bill. When you've done this, welcome family members to the future and have them return to their seats.

Share: Before we traveled into the future, I secretly placed each of your dollars into a special savings account or investment account. Now that we're here in the future, the money has earned what is called "interest" and is now worth two and a half times as much.

Age Adjustments

OLDER CHILDREN are often fascinated by the concept of investing. It's never too early to show them the long-term benefits of saving for retirement. Ask your older children to imagine how much money they'd end up with if they could put $500 into a savings account or another investment vehicle each year for thirty years. Then explain that if they earned an average of 10 percent in a tax-deferred account (not unreasonable for such a long period of time), they'd end up with nearly $90,000.

You may wish to explain to family members where the interest money came from. A simple way to do this is to say that the people you gave the dollars to agreed to pay you a little bit more if they could use the dollars while they kept them. Older children may wish to know more about how banks and other financial entities are able to pay money to savers and investors. A field trip to a bank or a visit with a financial planner could help them better understand the basics of saving and investing. Also, consider getting a copy of the book *Investing for the Future,* by Larry Burkett (Chariot Victor Publishing) to share with teens. Other money managing products for kids include: *Money Matters for Kids* by Lauree Burkett (Moody Press), *Money Matters for Teens, Money Matters for Teen workbooks* by Larry Burkett (Moody Press), Larry Burkett's Money Matters board game (age 12–adult) and Money Matters for Kids™ board game for ages 3–8 (Chariot Victor Publishing).

 Discuss these questions:
- **What were your reactions when you saw you had more money than before our "time travel" trip?** (I wondered where the other money came from; I was surprised because I expected the money to be gone.)
- **What does this exercise tell you about the value of saving or investing money?** (When we save, we can earn more; it doesn't take any work to make money when you invest.)
- **What would have been different in the future if you'd have spent the dollar on a toy or candy?** (We'd have nothing at all; we'd have no interest.)

Help family members see how different dollar amounts can accumulate over time using the simple formula of a beginning dollar amount times 2.5 (for a ten year investment at about 10 percent). When family members see that their $500 savings account could be worth $1,250, they'll certainly take notice and begin thinking about the benefits of saving.

If you haven't already done so, have family members stand and spin in the opposite direction to "return" to the present. If you can afford it (check your budget!), allow family members to keep the interest they "earned." Encourage them to add this money to their existing savings, or use it to begin a new savings or investment plan.

ACTIVITY 2: Time Flies

Point: Adding value to money through saving takes time.

 Supplies: You'll need supplies for making cookies and a Bible.

Share: When we think about the money we get, we usually think about ways to spend it. But we've learned that saving money can be a good thing because money can increase in value in savings accounts or through other investments. But there is one thing that we have to add to our money when we put it into an investment and that thing is time.

Explain that you're going to "invest" a little time in a family baking project. With your family members helping, follow the recipe for making some of your favorite cookies. Younger children will enjoy pouring ingredients into bowls and older children will enjoy dropping the cookie batter onto a cookie sheet. Make sure all family members participate in the cookie-making process.

When the first batch of cookies is in the oven, reconvene for a discussion time.

 Consider these questions:
  • **What was it like to work together to make cookies?** (It was fun; it was hard work; there was a lot of stuff to do.)
• **How is the work we did to make cookies like the work we do to get money (allowances, payment for odd jobs, etc)?** (We don't get money for nothing, we have to work for it—the same is true for cookies; we have to wait for our money just like we have to wait for cookies.)
• **Is it easy to wait for the cookies to be done? Why or why**

not? (No, I want them now; yes, I know they'll be good when they're done.)

Share: Waiting for these cookies to be done is like waiting for our savings or investments to earn us interest. It takes patience and time to see our investments grow. In a few minutes, we'll see the value of waiting as we enjoy some cookies. In a few years, we'll see the value of waiting if we've conducted wise saving and investing. (If your oven has a window, you might look in after a few minutes to see how the cookies have "grown.")

While the cookies are still cooking, summarize the story of Joseph's "saving plan" as outlined in Genesis 41. Here's a possible summary you could use: God gave Joseph wisdom to know what to do with his money. He had been raised as Jacob's favorite son, but he also worked for his grandfather, Laban. As he worked, Joseph learned that wealth is built gradually, bit by bit. When he was a slave, and even though he had no money of his own, Joseph managed every detail of Potiphar's house and, later, the prison. Both flourished. Joseph applied the principles of saving for future needs by not using up (or spending) everything he had.

 Then consider these questions:
- **What is the hardest thing about saving money?** (I like to spend it; it's hard to wait for things; I don't know where the money goes.)
- **What are some things we can do to be as wise as Joseph with our money?** (We can pray for God to help us; we can learn from other people who are good savers; we can save or invest as much as possible.)

When the cookies are done, remove them from the oven. Use the time while they're cooling to clean up the supplies used to make the cookies. Again, make sure every family member is included in the cleaning up process.

When the cookies are cool enough to eat, put some on a plate and set the plate in front of family members. You'll probably want some milk to go along with the cookies too. **Read** aloud Matthew 6:19-21.

Share: God wants us to be wise with our money. That means planning for the future by doing what Joseph did—saving and investing. But God also wants us to be sure we don't think about money too much. That's what this Bible passage tell us—we should focus on God and

not on money. **If we invest all our money and do everything we can to earn more, but we don't seek God's wisdom on how to do this and what to do with our money, all of our riches will be worth nothing.**

Have family members take a moment to thank God for the cookies, and to pray for wisdom to know how to save and invest their money. Then enjoy the cookies (and milk) and celebrate the value of being patient and how good things come to those who wait—and to those who save and invest their money.

WRAP-UP

Gather everyone in a circle and have family members take turns answering this question: **What's one thing you've learned about God today?**

Next, tell kids you've got a new "Life Slogan" you'd like to share with them.

Life Slogan: Today's Life Slogan is this: "Put money away for another day." Have family members repeat the slogan two or three times to help them learn it. Then encourage them to practice saying it during the week so they can talk about it at your next family night session.

Close in Prayer: Allow time for each family member to share prayer concerns and answers to prayer. Then close your time together with prayer for each concern. Thank God for listening to and caring about us.

Remember to record your prayer requests so you can refer to them in the future as you see God answering them.

⊚ 11: Spending

Exploring how to make wise spending decisions

Scripture
- Luke 15:11-32—Jesus tells the story of the Prodigal Son.
- Proverbs 31:16—The wise woman buys a field from her earnings.
- Matthew 6:21—Where one's treasure is, one's heart is too.

ACTIVITY OVERVIEW		
Activity	**Summary**	**Pre-Session Prep**
Activity 1: Need or Want?	Make a list of things they might want to purchase, then determine if they're needs or wants.	You'll need paper, pencils, glasses of drinking water, and a soft drink.
Activity 2: Shop 'til You Drop, but Don't Spend 'til the End.	Spend money to purchase food for a day's worth of family meals.	You'll need money and a Bible.

Main Points:

—There is a difference between needs and wants.

—Wise spending means getting good value from what we buy.

LIFE SLOGAN: "If you spend with care, your cupboards won't be bare."

Make it your own
In the space provided below, outline the flow and add any additional ideas to guide you through the process of conducting this family night.

Prayer & Praise Items
In the space provided below, list any items you wish to pray about or give praise for during this family night session.

Journal
In the space provided below, capture a record of any fun or meaningful things which happened during this family night session.

Session Tip

We intentionally have provided more material than we would expect to be used in a single "Family Night" session. You know your family's unique interests and life circumstances best, so feel free to adapt this lesson to meet your family members' needs. Remember, short and simple is better than long and comprehensive.

WARM-UP

Open with Prayer: Begin by having a family member pray, asking God to help everyone in the family understand more about Him through this time. After prayer, review your last lesson by asking these questions:

- What did we learn about in our last lesson?
- What was the Life Slogan?
- Have your actions changed because of what we learned? If so, how? Encourage family members to give specific examples of how they've applied learning from the past week.

Share: Today we're going to take a look at how we can be wise spenders.

ACTIVITY 1: Need or Want?

Point: There is a difference between needs and wants. Proverbs 31:16 and Matthew 6:21

Supplies: You'll need paper, pencils, glasses of drinking water, and a soft drink.

Activity: Place one glass of cold water on the table for each family member. In the center of the table, place a glass filled with a favorite soft drink. Ask family members to act out what life would be like if they didn't have any soft drinks (then go and pour the drink into the sink). If your family enjoys frequent or even occasional soft drinks, the responses could range from "oh, well" to expressions of mock panic.

Then have family members act out what life would be like without water—or any liquid that has water in it. Responses could range from clutching at the throat and crying for water to falling on the floor in mock death.

? Bring everyone back to "life" with a drink from their glass of water. Then discuss these questions:
- **What is the difference between water and a soft drink?** (Water doesn't taste as good; water is a need, soft drinks are wants.)
- **If you had to choose between unlimited glasses of water for a week or one six-pack of a favorite soft drink, which would you choose and why?** (The water, because I'd get thirsty a lot; the soft drinks because I like them better; the water, because it would last longer.)

Share: We can survive without soft drinks because our bodies don't need soft drinks to keep us alive. But if we didn't have water (including the water in soft drinks and other drinks), we couldn't survive. This illustrates the difference between needs and wants or necessities and frills. Let's look at this difference in another way.

Give each family member a sheet of paper and a pencil, pen, or crayon. Have each person list or draw a picture of the things they touch or use in a typical day—everything from their beds to the food they eat to their toys. Then help children circle the items on their lists that are needs. For example, someone might circle an item of clothing, because clothing is necessary for our society. Other things that might be circled could include a bed, a Bible, and other items. Remember that what some people consider to be a "need" could be considered a luxury to someone in a different socioeconomic situation.

Note

If your family doesn't drink soft drinks, choose other items to illustrate this difference between need and want. For example, we need the vitamins and nutrients in bread, fruit, and vegetables (among other things), but cookies and other treats, however tasty, are "want-based" foods, not necessary for our survival.

Age Adjustments

OLDER CHILDREN AND TEENAGERS can take this discussion further. For many older children, the peer pressure to have a certain kind of shoes or clothes causes them to move away from necessity-based purchases into the land of luxury. While a smart budget and good planning can help children afford these "wants" instead of the more cost-effective alternatives, it's appropriate for you to spend a little time talking with your older children about whether these things are truly needs or wants. While it may not be necessary to rule out the luxury items, it is important that children see the importance of taking care of more important needs before spending lots of money on a luxury.

Then discuss the following questions:

- **If you had a limited amount of money to spend, and you owned nothing, which things on your list would you buy first?** (The bed; a house; something to wear.)
- **What does this paper tell us about the way we spend our money?** (Most is spent on "wants"; we really don't have many things we have to buy.)

After your discussion, **share: A wise spender doesn't use all of his money for "wants" or luxuries before taking care of the needs. To be wise spenders, we must first take care of the things that are most important, and then we can think about buying some of the things that are wants.**

ACTIVITY 2: Shop 'til You Drop, but Don't Spend 'til the End.

Point: Wise spending means getting good value from what we buy.

 Supplies: You'll need money and a Bible.

Activity: For this activity, you'll need to go to a grocery store. Each family member will need enough money to purchase a day's worth of meal foods (one breakfast, lunch, and dinner). Choose an amount that will give family members a challenge and cause them to make difficult decisions regarding how to spread out the money. A figure of $15 could be a good challenge for many families.

Before going to the store, explain the rules of the game as follows:

- You only need to buy main items of food—condiments and seasonings can be used from the supplies we have at home.
- You must provide all the ingredients for sit-down meals for the entire family.
- Fruit, meat, vegetables, breads, and dairy products must be represented in at least one of the meals.
- Dessert items are optional—depending on how much money is left over after initial spending.

Give each family member paper, a pencil, and the appropriate amount of money. Grab a pocket calculator and head out to the store together. You'll want to have a parent go along with younger children to help them make their choices. Very young children can play a different game while at the store (see Age Adjustments).

It may be difficult to spend money on some items because of portion size. For example, if someone wants to buy potatoes for supper but they only come in five-pound bags, decide if you can use the rest of the potatoes and use a calculator to determine approximately how much of the cost should be added to the family member's total.

When everyone has purchased their food items, go back home and have each person present what he or she bought. Allow discussion about the purchases to include both praise for good ideas and constructive criticism of things that could have been done differently. Also, make plans for which days each of the family members' purchases will be used in family meal times.

Read aloud the story of the Prodigal Son, found in Luke 15:11-32 (or summarize it, paying special attention to the way the Prodigal Son spent his inheritance).

Then consider these questions:
- **How easy or difficult was it to buy items for a day's worth of meals?** (It was tough; it was easy because I found cheap foods; it was impossible.)
- **How is the way you made your decisions an example of wise or unwise spending?** (Buying cheaper foods was a wise choice; trying to buy my favorite foods was not very wise; I made a wise decision when I put back the ice cream.)
- **What was unwise about the way the Prodigal Son spent his money?** (He used it all on stupid things; he threw it away; he spent it on things he didn't need.)
- **Is it wrong to buy things that aren't needs? Why or why not?** (No, but we should take care of needs first; sometimes, if we could use the money for better things.)

Share: The Prodigal Son wasted his money on things that weren't necessary and so he ended up with nothing—looking for someone who could give him essential things like food and water. But wise

Age Adjustments

FOR YOUNGER CHILDREN, you can play a simple version of this shopping game by asking them to see how many candies they can buy with a dollar or two. Help them by doing the math as they run from bin to bin asking "how many of these can I get?" When they've purchased their candies, help them to discover that one dollar or two can be spent a lot of different ways, and that wise spenders sometimes need to get the most for their money.

OLDER CHILDREN AND TEENAGERS can learn wise spending habits when they're purchasing clothes. Whether you give them money to spend or they earn it themselves, take the opportunity next time they shop for clothes to remind them of the importance of wise shopping.

spenders look for good value and make sure they take care of needs before wants.

WRAP-UP

Gather everyone in a circle and have family members take turns answering this question: **What's one thing you've learned about God today?**

Next, tell kids you've got a new "Life Slogan" you'd like to share with them.

Life Slogan: Today's Life Slogan is this: "If you spend with care, your cupboards won't be bare." Have family members repeat the slogan two or three times to help them learn it. Then encourage them to practice saying it during the week so they can talk about it at your next family night session.

Close in Prayer: Allow time for each family member to share prayer concerns and answers to prayer. Then close your time together with prayer for each concern. Thank God for listening to and caring about us.

Remember to record your prayer requests so you can refer to them in the future as you see God answering them.

12: Debt and Credit

Exploring how patience can help us avoid debt

Scripture
- 2 Kings 4:1-7—A widow worries that her sons will be repayment for debt owed.
- Proverbs 22:7; Psalm 37:21—The borrower is servant to the lender.
- Romans 13:7-8—Leave no debt except love.

ACTIVITY OVERVIEW		
Activity	Summary	Pre-Session Prep
Activity 1: Are We in Debt Yet?	Play a game to explore what it means to be in debt.	You'll need magazines, advertisements, paper, a pencil, and a Bible.
Activity 2: Give What?	Learn how difficult it is to give to God and others when saddled with debt.	You'll need pennies or other coins.

Main Points:

—It's better to wait for something than to borrow money to buy it.

—It's difficult to be a giver when you're in debt.

LIFE SLOGAN: "Spending more than you own makes you slave to a loan."

Make it your own
In the space provided below, outline the flow and add any additional ideas to guide you through the process of conducting this family night.

Prayer & Praise Items
In the space provided below, list any items you wish to pray about or give praise for during this family night session.

Journal
In the space provided below, capture a record of any fun or meaningful things which happened during this family night session.

WARM-UP

Open with Prayer: Begin by having a family member pray, asking God to help everyone in the family understand more about Him through this time. After prayer, review your last lesson by asking these questions:

- **What did we learn about in our last lesson?**
- **What was the Life Slogan?**
- **Have your actions changed because of what we learned? If so, how?** Encourage family members to give specific examples of how they've applied learning from the past week.

Share: Today we're going to talk about what debt and credit are—and learn why it's usually better to wait for things until we can afford them than borrow money to get them right away.

ACTIVITY 1: Are We in Debt Yet?

Point: It's better to wait for something than to borrow money to buy it.

 Supplies: You'll need magazines, advertisements, paper, a pencil, and a Bible.

Activity: Collect a bunch of magazines and advertisements that might include things family members would like to have someday. For example, younger children might like to get a new bicycle, while older children might want their own computer or even a car. Set the periodicals on the floor and have each family member choose five things they'd like to have and tear out those pictures.

Then write a number (25, 50, or 100) on each item, based on its relative cost. For example, you might write a "25" on a smaller item such as a skateboard and a "100" on a more expensive item such as a car.

Ask family members to each choose one, two, or three of the items from their pictures that they'd like to purchase. Then add up the total amount they'd need in order to purchase those items. Explain that since they don't have any money right now, they could choose to wait one week for each number in their total (e.g.125 weeks for items totaling 125 points) to get their items, or get the items today if they borrow the money. If no one chooses to borrow money, ask why and then discuss how easy or difficult it is to wait for things you want to have. If people choose to borrow, give them their pictures, and then explain that they'll need to pay back an amount equal to twice the cost of the item, divided into monthly payments.

 Consider these questions:
- **What were your reactions if you chose to borrow when I told you you'd pay twice as much for your purchases?** (It didn't matter, I wanted them today anyway; I was surprised at how much I would have to pay.)
- **Would these items be worth spending twice their value on just to have them right now? Why or why not?** (No, I could use the extra money for something else; yes, if I had that bicycle today I could enjoy it longer.)

Age Adjustments

YOUNGER CHILDREN will enjoy a simpler version of this activity. Give each child five pennies. Then tell them they can buy a candy for ten pennies. Ask if they'd like to borrow five pennies so they could buy the candy now, or wait a half hour until they get five more pennies that they could use to buy the candy. If they choose to wait, give them five pennies in a half hour and allow them to buy the candy. If they choose to borrow, give them five pennies so they can buy the candy, then take the five pennies and a piece of the candy as your payment. Explain that when we borrow money, we have to pay back more than the item cost. Many children will think that waiting a half hour to get a whole candy is better than getting a partial candy right away.

After your discussion, **share: When we borrow money to get something, we go into debt. That means we owe somebody money. But going into debt doesn't just mean we need to pay the cost of the item back to the person we borrowed the money from—we also pay interest. In this case, unlike in saving and investing, interest is a bad thing since it's money we have to give to someone else.**

Read aloud 2 Kings 4:1-7. Explain this story if necessary to younger children. Help them see that because the man owed someone money, his wife was going to have to give up her sons as repayment. Assure younger children that this doesn't happen today, but that the lesson is still true: there are consequences when we borrow money.

Read aloud Proverbs 22:7, then **share: Whenever possible, we should wait until we have enough money to buy the things we need so we don't have to give even more money**

to a lender. As long as we owe a lender money, we end up serving them rather than taking care of our own financial needs. Try using a layaway plan rather than a credit card.

ACTIVITY 2: Give What?

Point: It's difficult to be a giver when you're a debtor.

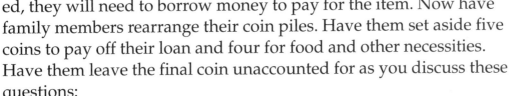

Supplies: You'll need pennies or other coins.

Activity: Give each person ten pennies or other coins. Explain that this money represents what they might get for an allowance or in a weekly paycheck. Have family members divide their coins into the following piles: one coin for tithe; two coins for saving; four coins for food and other necessities; and three coins for spending. Now ask family members to imagine they just saw the greatest new video game, toy, shirt, shoes, or whatever, that they just have to have today. Since their savings is just getting started, they will need to borrow money to pay for the item. Now have family members rearrange their coin piles. Have them set aside five coins to pay off their loan and four for food and other necessities. Have them leave the final coin unaccounted for as you discuss these questions:

- **How will you use the only coin you have left?** (Spending; saving; church.)
- **How has your loan affected your ability to give to the church and others?** (I have the same amount of money, but none for myself; I wouldn't have enough to give.)

Share: When we borrow money, sometimes we jeopardize other things we should be using our money for. Many people have so much debt (or money that they owe) that they don't have any left over to give as a tithe. While we know from our family night activities on tithing that a tithe should be the first place we use our money, sometimes people overspend and choose not to tithe just so they have food to eat or clothes to wear.

Age Adjustments

FOR OLDER CHILDREN AND TEENAGERS, add a discussion of the following Scriptures that explore debt: Psalm 37:21; Luke 6:34-35; Romans 13:8. Have your children respond to each passage and determine how the message of the passage might apply to them.

It's important to use money wisely so we can be sure to give our tithe, pay for necessary items like food and clothes, and save for times when we might need more money. That's why borrowing money isn't usually a good idea.

You may wish to add an addendum to this discussion describing why people frequently take out a loan for a first house, or even a car in many cases. When talking about necessary debt or loans, help your children to understand that they should never borrow more money than they can pay back.

An additional discussion on what a credit card is may be appropriate here for older children. Here are a few points that children ought to know about credit cards:

- It's easy to use credit cards to pay for things.
- Most credit cards allow you to pay back the amount you spend on them without any additional interest if you pay within 20 to 30 days.
- Using a credit card isn't a bad thing if you always pay back the entire amount spent each month when the bill comes.
- If you don't pay back what you've spent each month, you'll end up paying more money back in interest and quickly dig yourself into debt.
- Never spend money on a credit card that you didn't already have budgeted in your regular budget. That way, when the bill comes, you'll be able to pay it right **away.**

WRAP-UP

Gather everyone in a circle and have family members take turns answering this question: **What's one thing you've learned about God today?**

Next, tell kids you've got a new "Life Slogan" you'd like to share with them.

Life Slogan: Today's Life Slogan is this: "Spending more than you own makes you slave to a loan." Have family members repeat the slogan two or three times to help them learn it. Then encourage them to practice saying it during the week so they can talk about it at your next family night session.

 Close in Prayer: Allow time for each family member to share prayer concerns and answers to prayer. Then close your time together with prayer for each concern. Thank God for listening to and caring about us.

Remember to record your prayer requests so you can refer to them in the future as you see God answering them.

Additional Resources

For Parents and Young Adults:

105 Questions Children Ask about Money Matters, by Rick Osborne
The Complete Financial Guide for Young Couples, by Larry Burkett
Debt-Free Living, by Larry Burkett
Financial Parenting, by Larry Burkett & Rick Osborne
The Financial Planning Workbook, by Larry Burkett
How to Manage Your Money, by Larry Burkett
Investing for the Future, by Larry Burkett
Money Management for College Students, by Larry Burkett
Your Finances in Changing Times, by Larry Burkett

For Younger Kids and Teens:

50 Money Making Ideas for Kids, by Allen & Lauree Burkett
Larry Burkett's Money Matters board game, ages 8 and up
Money Matters for Kids, by Allen & Lauree Burkett
Money Matters for Kids board game, ages 4-12
Money Matters for Teens, by Allen and Lauree Burkett
Money Matters for Teens Workbook, Age 11-14 Edition, by Larry Burkett
   with Todd Temple
Money Matters for Teens Workbook, Age 15-18 Edition, by Larry Burkett
   with Todd Temple
My Giving Bank, ages 3 and up
What If I Owned Everything? by Larry Burkett & Lauree Burkett

℮ How to Lead Your Child to Christ

SOME THINGS TO CONSIDER AHEAD OF TIME:

1. Realize that God is more concerned about your child's eternal destiny and happiness than you are. "The Lord is not slow in keeping His promise. . . . He is patient with you, not wanting anyone to perish, but everyone to come to repentance" (2 Peter 3:9).

2. Pray specifically beforehand that God will give you insights and wisdom in dealing with each child on his or her maturity level.

3. Don't use terms like "take Jesus into your heart," "dying and going to hell," and "accepting Christ as your personal Savior." Children are either too literal ("How does Jesus breathe in my heart?") or the words are too clichéd and trite for their understanding.

4. Deal with each child alone, and don't be in a hurry. Make sure he or she understands. Discuss. Take your time.

A FEW CAUTIONS:

1. When drawing children to Himself, Jesus said for others to "allow" them to come to Him (see Mark 10:14). Only with adults did He use the term "compel" (see Luke 14:23). Do not compel children.

2. Remember that unless the Holy Spirit is speaking to the child, there will be no genuine heart experience of regeneration. Parents, don't get caught up in the idea that Jesus will return the day before you were going to speak to your child about salvation and that it will be too late. Look at God's character— He *is* love! He is not dangling your child's soul over hell. Wait on God's timing.

    Pray with faith, believing. Be concerned, but don't push.

THE PLAN:

1. **God loves you.** Recite John 3:16 with your child's name in place of "the world."

2. **Show the child his or her need of a Savior.**

   a. Deal with sin carefully. There is one thing that cannot enter heaven—sin.

   b. Be sure your child knows what sin is. Ask him to name some (things common to children—lying, sassing, disobeying, etc.). Sin is doing or thinking anything wrong according to God's Word. It is breaking God's Law.

   c. Ask the question "Have you sinned?" If the answer is no, do not continue. Urge him to come and talk to you again when he does feel that he has sinned. Dismiss him. You may want to have prayer first, however, thanking God "for this young child who is willing to do what is right." Make it easy for him to talk to you again, but do not continue. Do not say, "Oh, yes, you have too sinned!" and then name some. With children, wait for God's conviction.

   d. If the answer is yes, continue. He may even give a personal illustration of some sin he has done recently or one that has bothered him.

   e. Tell him what God says about sin: We've all sinned ("There is no one righteous, not even one," Rom. 3:10). And because of that sin, we can't get to God ("For the wages of sin is death . . . " Rom. 6:23). So He had to come to us (". . . but the gift of God is eternal life in Christ Jesus our Lord," Rom. 6:23).

   f. Relate God's gift of salvation to Christmas gifts—we don't earn them or pay for them; we just accept them and are thankful for them.

3. **Bring the child to a definite decision.**

   a. Christ must be received if salvation is to be possessed.

   b. Remember, do not force a decision.

   c. Ask the child to pray out loud in her own words. Give her some things she could say if she seems unsure. Now be prepared for a blessing! (It is best to avoid having the child repeat a memorized prayer after you. Let her think, and make it personal.)*

d. After salvation has occurred, pray for her out loud. This is a good way to pronounce a blessing on her.

4. **Lead your child into assurance.**

Show him that he will have to keep his relationship open with God through repentance and forgiveness (just like with his family or friends), but that God will always love him ("Never will I leave you; never will I forsake you," Heb. 13:5).

* If you wish to guide your child through the prayer, here is some suggested language.

"Dear God, I know that I am a sinner [have child name specific sins he or she acknowledged earlier, such as lying, stealing, disobeying, etc.]. I know that Jesus died on the cross to pay for all my sins. I ask You to forgive me of my sins. I believe that Jesus died for me and rose from the dead, and I accept Him as my Savior. Thank You for loving me. In Jesus' name. Amen."

Cumulative Topical Index

TOPIC	SCRIPTURE	WHAT YOU'LL NEED	WHERE TO FIND IT
The Acts of the Sinful Nature and the Fruit of the Spirit	Gal. 5:19-26	3x5 cards or paper, markers, and tape	IFN, p. 43
Adding Value to Money through Saving Takes Time	Matt. 6:19-21	Supplies for making cookies and a Bible	MMK, p. 89
All Have Sinned	Rom. 3:23	Raw eggs, bucket of water	BCB, p. 89
All of Our Plans Should Match God's	Ps. 139:1-18	Paper, pencils, markers, or crayons	MMK, p. 73
Avoid Things That Keep Us from Growing	Eph. 4:14-15; Heb. 5:11-14	Seeds, plants at various stages of growth or a garden or nursery to tour, Bible	CCQ, p. 77
Bad Company Corrupts Good Character	1 Cor. 15:33	Small ball, string, slips of paper, pencil, yarn or masking tape, Bible	IFN, p. 103
Be Thankful for Good Friends		Bible, art supplies, markers	IFN, p. 98
Being Content with What We Have	Phil. 4:11-13	Bible	CCQ, p. 17
Being Diligent Means Working Hard and Well	Gen. 39–41	Bible, paper, a pencil and other supplies depending on jobs chosen	MMK, p. 64
Being a Faithful Steward Means Managing God's Gifts Wisely	1 Peter 4:10; Luke 19:12-26	Graham crackers, peanut butter, thin stick pretzels, small marshmallows, and M & Ms®	MMK, p. 18
Budgeting Means Making a Plan for Using Our Money	Jud. 6–7	Table, large sheets or paper, and markers or crayons	MMK, p. 79
Budgeting Means the Money Coming in Has to Equal the Money Going Out	Luke 14:28-35; Jud. 6–7	Supply of beans, paper, pencil, and Bible	MMK, p. 80
Change Helps Us Grow and Mature	Rom. 8:28-39	Bible	WLS, p. 39

TOPIC	SCRIPTURE	WHAT YOU'LL NEED	WHERE TO FIND IT
Change Is Good	1 Kings 17:8-16	Jar or box for holding change, colored paper, tape, markers, Bible	MMK, p. 27
Christ Is Who We Serve	Col. 3:23-24	Paper, scissors, pens	IFN, p. 50
Christians Should Be Joyful Each Day	James 3:22-23; Ps. 118:24	Small plastic bottle, cork to fit bottle opening, water, vinegar, paper towel, Bible	CCQ, p. 67
Commitment and Hard Work Are Needed to Finish Strong	Gen. 6:5-22	Jigsaw puzzle, Bible	CCQ, p. 83
The Consequence of Sin Is Death	Ps. 19:1-6	Dominoes	BCB, p. 57
Contentment Is the Secret to Happiness	Matt. 6:33	Package of candies, a Bible	MMK, p. 51
Creation	Gen. 1:1; Ps. 19:1-6; Rom. 1:20	Nature book or video, Bible	IFN, p. 17
David and Bathsheba	2 Sam. 11:1–12:14	Bible	BCB, p. 90
Description of Heaven	Rev. 21:3-4, 10-27	Bible, drawing supplies	BCB, p. 76
Difficulty Can Help Us Grow	Jer. 32:17; Luke 18:27	Bible, card game like Old Maid or Crazy Eights	CCQ, p. 33
Discipline and Training Make Us Stronger	Prov. 4:23	Narrow doorway, Bible	CCQ, p. 103
Don't Be Yoked with Unbelievers	2 Cor. 16:17–17:1	Milk, food coloring	IFN, p. 105
Don't Give Respect Based on Material Wealth	Eph. 6:1-8; 1 Peter 2:13-17; Ps. 119:17; James 2:1-2; 1 Tim. 4:12	Large sheet of paper, tape, a pen, Bible	IFN, p. 64
Equality Does Not Mean Contentment	Matt. 20:1-16	Money or candy bars, tape recorder or radio, Bible	WLS, p. 21
Even if We're Not in the Majority, We May Be Right	2 Tim. 3:12-17	Piece of paper, pencil, water	CCQ, p. 95
Every Day Is a Gift from God	Prov. 16:9	Bible	CCQ, p. 69
Evil Hearts Say Evil Words	Prov. 15:2-8; Luke 6:45; Eph. 4:29	Bible, small mirror	IFN, p. 79
The Fruit of the Spirit	Gal. 5:22-23; Luke 3:8; Acts 26:20	Blindfold and Bible	BCB, p. 92

TOPIC	SCRIPTURE	WHAT YOU'LL NEED	WHERE TO FIND IT
God Allows Testing to Help Us Mature	James 1:2-4	Bible	BCB, p. 44
God Can Clean Our Guilty Consciences	1 John 1:9	Small dish of bleach, dark piece of material, Bible	WLS, p. 95
God Can Do the Impossible	John 6:1-14	Bible, sturdy plank (6 or more inches wide and 6 to 8 feet long), a brick or similar object, snack of fish and crackers	CCQ, p. 31
God Can Guide Us Away from Satan's Traps	Ps. 119:9-11; Prov. 3:5-6	Ten or more inexpensive mousetraps, pencil, blindfold, Bible	WLS, p. 72
God Can Help Us Knock Sin Out of Our Lives	Ps. 32:1-5; 1 John 1:9	Heavy drinking glass, pie tin, small slips of paper, pencils, large raw egg, cardboard tube from a roll of toilet paper, broom, masking tape, Bible	WLS, p. 53
God Cares for Us Even in Hard Times	Job 1–2; 42	Bible	WLS, p. 103
God Created Us	Isa. 45:9, 64:8; Ps. 139:13	Bible and video of potter with clay	BCB, p. 43
God Doesn't Want Us to Worry	Matt. 6:25-34; Phil. 4:6-7; Ps. 55:22	Bible, paper, pencils	CCQ, p. 39
God Forgives Those Who Confess Their Sins	1 John 1:9	Sheets of paper, tape, Bible	BCB, p. 58
God Gave Jesus a Message for Us	John 1:14,18; 8:19; 12:49-50	Goldfish in water or bug in jar, water	BCB, p. 66
God Gives and God Can Take Away	Luke 12:13-21	Bible, timer with bell or buzzer, large bowl of small candies, smaller bowl for each child	CCQ, p. 15
God Is Holy	Ex. 3:1-6	Masking tape, baby powder or corn starch, broom, Bible	IFN, p. 31
God Is Invisible, Powerful, and Real	John 1:18, 4:24; Luke 24:36-39	Balloons, balls, refrigerator magnets, Bible	IFN, p. 15
God Knew His Plans for Us	Jer. 29:11	Two puzzles and a Bible	BCB, p. 19
God Knows All about Us	Ps. 139:2-4; Matt. 10:30	3x5 cards, a pen	BCB, p. 17
God Knows Everything	Isa. 40:13-14; Eph. 4:1-6	Bible	IFN, p. 15

Family Night
TOOL CHEST

AN
INTRODUCTION
TO FAMILY
NIGHTS
= IFN

BASIC
CHRISTIAN
BELIEFS
= BCB

CHRISTIAN
CHARACTER
QUALITIES
= CCQ

WISDOM LIFE
SKILLS
= WLS

MONEY
MATTERS FOR
KIDS
= MMK

TOPIC	SCRIPTURE	WHAT YOU'LL NEED	WHERE TO FIND IT
God Knows the Plan for Our Lives	Rom. 8:28	Three different 25–50 piece jigsaw puzzles, Bible	WLS, p. 101
God Loves Us So Much, He Sent Jesus	John 3:16; Eph. 2:8-9	I.O.U. for each family member	IFN, p. 34
God Made Our Family Unique by Placing Each of Us in It		Different color paint for each family member, toothpicks or paintbrushes to dip into paint, white paper, Bible	BCB, p. 110
God Made Us in His Image	Gen. 1:24-27	Play dough or clay and Bible	BCB, p. 24
God Never Changes	Ecc. 3:1-8; Heb. 13:8	Paper, pencils, Bible	WLS, p. 37
God Owns Everything; He Gives Us Things to Manage		Large sheet of poster board or newsprint and colored markers	MMK, p. 17
God Provides a Way Out of Temptation	1 Cor. 10:12-13; James 1:13-14; 4:7; 1 John 2:15-17	Bible	IFN, p. 88
God Wants Our Best Effort in All We Do	Col. 3:23-24	Children's blocks or a large supply of cardboard boxes	MMK, p. 63
God Wants Us to Be Diligent in Our Work	Prov. 6:6-11; 1 Thes. 4:11-12	Video about ants or picture books or encyclopedia, Bible	CCQ, p. 55
God Wants Us to Get Closer to Him	James 4:8; 1 John 4:7-12	Hidden Bibles, clues to find them	BCB, p. 33
God Wants Us to Glorify Him	Ps. 24:1; Luke 12:13-21	Paper, pencils, Bible	WLS, p. 47
God Wants Us to Work and Be Helpful	2 Thes. 3:6-15	Several undone chores, Bible	CCQ, p. 53
God Will Send the Holy Spirit	John 14:23-26; 1 Cor. 2:12	Flashlights, small treats, Bible	IFN, p. 39
God's Covenant with Noah	Gen. 8:13-21; 9:8-17	Bible, paper, crayons or markers	BCB, p. 52
Guarding the Gate to Our Minds	Prov. 4:13; 2 Cor. 11:3; Phil. 4:8	Bible, poster board for each family member, old magazines, glue, scissors, markers	CCQ, p. 23
The Holy Spirit Helps Us	Eph. 1:17; John 14:15-17; Acts 1:1-11; Eph. 3:16-17; Rom. 8:26-27; 1 Cor. 2:11-16	Bible	BCB, p. 99

TOPIC	SCRIPTURE	WHAT YOU'LL NEED	WHERE TO FIND IT
Honesty Means Being Sure We Tell the Truth and Are Fair	Prov. 10:9; 11:3; 12:5; 14:2; 28:13	A bunch of coins and a Bible	MMK, p. 58
Honor the Holy Spirit, Don't Block Him	1 John 4:4; 1 Cor. 6:19-20	Bible, blow-dryer or vacuum cleaner with exit hose, a Ping-Pong ball	CCQ, p. 47
Honor Your Parents	Ex. 20:12	Paper, pencil, treats, umbrella, soft objects, masking tape, pen, Bible	IFN, p. 55
Investing and Saving Adds Value to Money	Prov. 21:20	Two and a half dollars for each family member	MMK, p. 87
It's Better to Follow the Truth	Rom. 1:25; Prov. 2:1-5	Second set of clues, box of candy or treats, Bible	WLS, p. 86
It's Better to Wait for Something Than to Borrow Money to Buy It	2 Kings 4:1-7; Prov. 22:7	Magazines, advertisements, paper, a pencil, Bible	MMK, p. 103
It's Difficult to Be a Giver When You're a Debtor		Pennies or other coins	MMK, p. 105
It's Easy to Follow a Lie, but It Leads to Disappointment		Clues as described in lesson, empty box	WLS, p. 85
The Importance of Your Name Being Written in the Book of Life	Rev. 20:11-15; 21:27	Bible, phone book, access to other books with family name	BCB, p. 74
It's Important to Listen to Jesus' Message		Bible	BCB, p. 68
Jesus Dies on the Cross	John 14:6	6-foot 2x4, 3-foot 2x4, hammers, nails, Bible	IFN, p. 33
Jesus Took the Punishment We Deserve	Rom. 6:23; John 3:16; Rom. 5:8-9	Bathrobe, list of bad deeds	IFN, p. 26
Jesus Washes His Followers' Feet	John 13:1-17	Bucket of warm soapy water, towels, Bible	IFN, p. 63
Joshua and the Battle of Jericho	Josh. 1:16-18; 6:1-21	Paper, pencil, dots on paper that, when connected, form a star	IFN, p. 57
Knowing God's Word Helps Us Know What Stand to Take	2 Tim. 3:1-5	Current newspaper, Bible	CCQ, p. 93

Family Night
TOOL CHEST

AN INTRODUCTION TO FAMILY NIGHTS
= IFN

BASIC CHRISTIAN BELIEFS
= BCB

CHRISTIAN CHARACTER QUALITIES
= CCQ

WISDOM LIFE SKILLS
= WLS

MONEY MATTERS FOR KIDS
= MMK

TOPIC	SCRIPTURE	WHAT YOU'LL NEED	WHERE TO FIND IT
Look to God, Not Others	Phil. 4:11-13	Magazines or newspapers, a chair, several pads of small yellow stickies, Bible	WLS, p. 24
Loving Money Is Wrong	1 Tim. 6:6-10	Several rolls of coins, masking tape, Bible	WLS, p. 45
Lying Can Hurt People	Acts 5:1-11	Two pizza boxes—one empty and one with a fresh pizza—and a Bible	MMK, p. 57
Meeting Goals Requires Planning	Prov. 3:5-6	Paper, scissors, pencils, a treat, a Bible	MMK, p. 71
The More We Know God, the More We Know His Voice	John 10:1-6	Bible	BCB, p. 35
Nicodemus Asks Jesus about Being Born Again	John 3:7, 50-51; 19:39-40	Bible, paper, pencil, costume	BCB, p. 81
Obedience Has Good Rewards		Planned outing everyone will enjoy, directions on 3x5 cards, number cards	IFN, p. 59
Only a Relationship with God Can Fill Our Need	Isa. 55:1-2	Doll that requires batteries, batteries for the doll, dollar bill, pictures of a house, an expensive car, and a pretty woman or handsome man, Bible	WLS, p. 62
Our Conscience Helps Us Know Right from Wrong	Rom. 2:14-15	Foods with a strong smell, blindfold, Bible	WLS, p. 93
Our Minds Should Be Filled with Good, Not Evil	Phil 4:8; Ps. 119:9, 11	Bible, bucket of water, several large rocks	CCQ, p. 26
Parable of the Talents	Matt. 25:14-30	Bible	IFN, p. 73
Parable of the Vine and Branches	John 15:1-8	Tree branch, paper, pencils, Bible	IFN, p. 95
Persecution Brings a Reward		Bucket, bag of ice, marker, one-dollar bill	WLS, p. 32
Planning Helps Us Finish Strong	Phil. 3:10-14	Flight map on p. 86, paper, pencils, Bible	CCQ, p. 85
Pray, Endure, and Be Glad When We're Persecuted	Matt. 5:11-12, 44; Rom. 12:14; 1 Cor. 4:12	Notes, Bible, candle or flashlight, dark small space	WLS, p. 29
The Responsibilities of Families	Eph. 5:22-33; 6:1-4	Photo albums, Bible	BCB, p. 101

TOPIC	SCRIPTURE	WHAT YOU'LL NEED	WHERE TO FIND IT
Satan Looks for Ways to Trap Us	Luke 4:1-13	Cardboard box, string, stick, small ball, Bible	WLS, p. 69
Self-control Helps Us Resist the Enemy	1 Peter 5:8-9; 1 Peter 2:11-12	Blindfold, watch or timer, feather or other "tickly" item, Bible	CCQ, p. 101
Serve One Another in Love	Gal. 5:13	Bag of small candies, at least three per child	IFN, p. 47
Sin and Busyness Interfere with Our Prayers	Luke 10:38-42; Ps. 46:10; Matt. 5:23-24; 1 Peter 3:7	Bible, two paper cups, two paper clips, long length of fishing line	CCQ, p. 61
Sin Separates Humanity	Gen. 3:1-24	Bible, clay creations, piece of hardened clay or play dough	BCB, p. 25
Some Places Aren't Open to Everyone		Book or magazine with "knock-knock" jokes	BCB, p. 73
Some Things in Life Are Out of Our Control		Blindfolds	BCB, p. 41
Temptation Takes Our Eyes Off God		Fishing pole, items to catch, timer, Bible	IFN, p. 85
There Is a Difference between Needs and Wants	Prov. 31:16; Matt. 6:21	Paper, pencils, glasses of drinking water, a soft drink	MMK, p. 95
Those Who Don't Believe Are Foolish	Ps. 44:1	Ten small pieces of paper, pencil, Bible	IFN, p. 19
Tithing Means Giving One-Tenth Back to God	Gen. 28:10-22; Ps. 3:9-10	All family members need ten similar items each, a Bible	MMK, p. 33
The Tongue Is Small but Powerful	James 3:3-12	Video, news magazine or picture book showing devastation of fire, match, candle, Bible	IFN, p. 77
Trials Help Us Grow	James 1:2-4	Sugar cookie dough, cookie cutters, baking sheets, miscellaneous baking supplies, Bible	WLS, p. 15
Trials Test How We've Grown	James 1:12	Bible	WLS, p. 17
Trust Is Important	Matt. 6:25-34	Each person needs an item he or she greatly values	MMK, p. 25
We All Sin	Rom. 3:23	Target and items to throw	IFN, p. 23

Family Night
TOOL CHEST

AN INTRODUCTION TO FAMILY NIGHTS
= **IFN**

BASIC CHRISTIAN BELIEFS
= **BCB**

CHRISTIAN CHARACTER QUALITIES
= **CCQ**

WISDOM LIFE SKILLS
= **WLS**

MONEY MATTERS FOR KIDS
= **MMK**

AN
INTRODUCTION
TO FAMILY
NIGHTS
= IFN

BASIC
CHRISTIAN
BELIEFS
= BCB

CHRISTIAN
CHARACTER
QUALITIES
= CCQ

WISDOM LIFE
SKILLS
= WLS

MONEY
MATTERS FOR
KIDS
= MMK

TOPIC	SCRIPTURE	WHAT YOU'LL NEED	WHERE TO FIND IT
We Can Communicate with Each Other			BCB, p. 65
We Can Fight the Temptation to Want More Stuff	Matt. 4:1-11; Heb. 13:5	Television, paper, a pencil, Bible	MMK, p. 49
We Can Give Joyfully to Others	Luke 10:25-37	Bible, soft yarn	MMK, p. 41
We Can Help Each Other	Prov. 27:17	Masking tape, bowl of unwrapped candies, rulers, yardsticks, or dowel rods	BCB, p. 110
We Can Help People When We Give Generously	2 Cor. 6–7	Variety of supplies, depending on chosen activity	MMK, p. 43
We Can Love by Helping Those in Need	Heb. 13:1-3		IFN, p. 48
We Can Show Love through Respecting Family Members		Paper and pen	IFN, p. 66
We Can't Take Back the Damage of Our Words		Tube of toothpaste for each child, $10 bill	IFN, p. 78
We Deserve Punishment for Our Sins	Rom. 6:23	Dessert, other materials as decided	IFN, p. 24
We Give to God because We're Thankful		Supplies for a celebration dinner, also money for each family member	MMK, p. 36
We Have All We Need in Our Lives	Ecc. 3:11	Paper, pencils, Bible	WLS, p. 61
We Have a New Life in Christ	John 3:3; 2 Cor. 5:17	Video or picture book of caterpillar forming a cocoon then a butterfly, or a tadpole becoming a frog, or a seed becoming a plant	BCB, p. 93
We Know Others by Our Relationships with Them		Copies of questionnaire, pencils, Bible	BCB, p. 31
We Must Be in Constant Contact with God		Blindfold	CCQ, p. 63
We Must Choose to Obey		3x5 cards or slips of paper, markers, and tape	IFN, p. 43
We Must Either Choose Christ or Reject Christ	Matt. 12:30	Clear glass jar, cooking oil, water, spoon, Bible	CCQ, p. 96

TOPIC	SCRIPTURE	WHAT YOU'LL NEED	WHERE TO FIND IT
We Must Learn How Much Responsibility We Can Handle		Building blocks, watch with second hand, paper, pencil	IFN, p. 71
We Must Listen	Prov. 1:5, 8-9; 4:1	Bible, other supplies for the task you choose	WLS, p. 77
We Must Think Before We Speak	James 1:19	Bible	WLS, p. 79
We Need to Grow Physically, Emotionally, and Spiritually	1 Peter 2:2	Photograph albums or videos of your children at different ages, tape measure, bathroom scale, Bible	CCQ, p. 75
We Reap What We Sow	Gal. 6:7	Candy bar, Bible	IFN, p. 55
We Shouldn't Value Possessions Over Everything Else	1 Tim. 6:7-8	Box is optional	CCQ, p. 18
Wise Spending Means Getting Good Value for What We Buy	Luke 15:11-32	Money and a Bible	MMK, p. 97
With Help, Life Is a Lot Easier		Supplies to do the chore you choose	BCB, p. 101
Wolves in Sheeps' Clothing	Matt. 7:15-20	Ten paper sacks, a marker, ten small items, Bible	IFN, p. 97
Worrying Doesn't Change Anything		Board, inexpensive doorbell buzzer, a 9-volt battery, extra length of electrical wire, a large belt, assorted tools	CCQ, p. 37
You Look Like the Person in Whose Image You Are Created		Paper roll, crayons, markers, pictures of your kids and of yourself as a child	BCB, p. 23

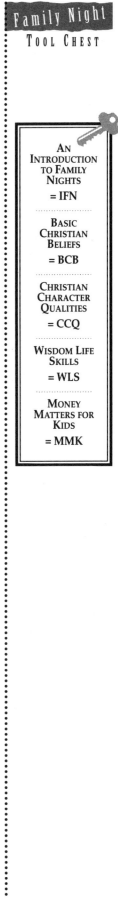

Family Night
TOOL CHEST

AN INTRODUCTION TO FAMILY NIGHTS
= IFN

BASIC CHRISTIAN BELIEFS
= BCB

CHRISTIAN CHARACTER QUALITIES
= CCQ

WISDOM LIFE SKILLS
= WLS

MONEY MATTERS FOR KIDS
= MMK

About Heritage Builders

OUR VISION

To build a network of families, churches, and individuals committed to passing a strong family heritage to the next generation and to support one another in that effort.

OUR VALUES

Family—We believe that the traditional, intact family provides the most stable and healthy environment for passing a strong heritage to the next generation, but that non-intact homes can also successfully pass a solid heritage.

Faith—We believe that many of the principles for passing a solid heritage are effective regardless of one's religious tradition, but that the Christian faith provides the only lasting foundation upon which to build a strong family heritage.

Values—We believe that there are certain moral absolutes which govern our world and serve as the foundation upon which a strong heritage should be built, and that the current trend toward value neutrality is unraveling the heritage fabric of future generations.

Church—We believe that all families need a support network and that the local church is the institution of choice for helping families successfully pass a strong heritage to the next generation.

OUR BELIEFS

We embrace the essential tenets of orthodox Christianity as summarized by the National Association of Evangelicals:

1. We believe the Bible to be the inspired, the only infallible, authoritative Word of God.

2. We believe that there is one God, eternally existent in three persons: Father, Son, and Holy Ghost.

3. *We believe in the deity of our Lord Jesus Christ, in His virgin birth, in His sinless life, in His miracles, in His vicarious and atoning death through His shed blood, in His bodily resurrection, in His ascension to the right hand of the Father, and in His personal return in power and glory.*

4. *We believe that for the salvation of lost and sinful people, regeneration by the Holy Spirit is absolutely essential.*

5. *We believe in the present ministry of the Holy Spirit, by whose indwelling the Christian is enabled to live a godly life.*

6. *We believe in the resurrection of both the saved and the lost; they that are saved unto the resurrection of life and they that are lost unto the resurrection of damnation.*

7. *We believe in the spiritual unity of believers in our Lord Jesus Christ.*

OUR PEOPLE

Heritage Builders is lead by a team of family life experts.

Cofounder - J. Otis Ledbetter, Ph.D.
Married over 25 years to Gail, two grown children, one teenager
Pastor, Chestnut Baptist Church in Clovis, California
Author - *The Heritage, Family Fragrance, Family Traditions*

Cofounder - Kurt Bruner, M.A.
Married over 12 years to Olivia, three young sons
Vice President, Focus on the Family Resource Group
Author - *The Heritage, Family Night Tool Chest* Series

Cofounder - Jim Weidmann
Married over 15 years to Janet, two sons, two daughters
Family Night Training Consultant
Author - *Family Night Tool Chest* Series

Senior Associates - Heritage Builders draws upon the collective wisdom of various authors, teachers, and parents who provide resources, motivation, and advice for the heritage passing process.

BECOME A HERITAGE BUILDER IN YOUR COMMUNITY!

We seek to fulfill our mission by sponsoring the following.

HERITAGE BUILDERS RESOURCES - Products specifically designed to motivate and assist parents in the heritage passing process.

HERITAGE WORKSHOP - Using various formats, this seminar teaches attendees the principles and tools for passing a solid heritage, and helps them create a highly practical action plan for doing so.

HERITAGE BUILDERS NETWORK - A network of churches which have established an ongoing heritage builder support ministry where families can help families through mutual encouragement and creativity.

HERITAGE BUILDERS NEWSLETTER - We provide a forum through which families can share heritage building success stories and tips in our periodic newsletter.

If you are interested in hosting a Heritage Workshop, launching a Heritage Builders ministry in your local church, learning about new Heritage Building resources, receiving our newsletter, or becoming a Heritage Builder Associate, contact us by writing, phoning, or visiting our web site.

Heritage Builders Association
c/o Chariot Victor Publishing
4050 Lee Vance View
Colorado Springs, CO 80918
or call: 1-800-528-9489 (7 A.M.– 4:30 P.M. MST)
www.chariotvictor.com
or
www.heritagebuilders.com

HERITAGE BUILDERS

☐ Please send me a FREE One-Year Subscription to Heritage Builders Newsletter.

Name _____

Address _____

City _____ State _____ Zip _____ Phone _____

Church Affiliation _____

E-mail Address _____

Signature _____